Learning and Memory

Learning and Memory

Donald A. Norman

University of California at San Diego

W. H. Freeman and Company
San Francisco

Project Editor: Judith Wilson
Copy Editor: Pat Lauber
Designer: Gary Head
Production Coordinator: Bill Murdock
Art Coordinator: Richard Quiñones
Artist: Patricia Goff Design
Compositor: Vera Allen Composition
Printer and Binder: The Maple-Vail Book Manufacturing Group

Library of Congress Cataloging in Publication Data

Norman, Donald A.
Learning and memory.

Bibliography: p.
Includes index.
1. Memory.   2. Artificial intelligence.   3. Learning, Psychology of.   I. Title.
BF371.N568   153.1   82-7441
ISBN 0-7167-1299-7   AACR2
ISBN 0-7167-1300-4 (pbk.)

This is for Cynthia and Michael

Contents

Preface

Once upon a time, in the dimly remembered past, I was visited by Edmund H. Immergut, a chemist, I was told. What could he want of me, I wondered. A book, he explained, a simple, short book on human learning and memory for the "noncaptive" reader, a book that could also serve to captivate undergraduates studying cognition, learning and memory, and artificial intelligence. It would be necessary to discuss memory storage, processing, semantic networks, schemas, and to discuss these topics in a way that would be accessible to readers varying widely in background and motivation.

I did not anticipate that it would take so long to write a "simple" book. We have been in a period of very active research, and the topics I thought I would write about have been superseded by more comprehensive views, by a better appreciation for the functioning of humans, and by an increasing awareness of the gaps in our knowledge. Our findings have been exciting, leading to new conceptualizations and a broadening of our understanding of mental structures. But how could I capture the rapidly advancing research, and, moreover, capture it at just the right intellectual level for the intended reader?

Eventually there was no choice but to stop everything else and write the book. The result is a personal selection of some of the issues of psychological research that may lead the reader to broader topics. I have tried to provide insight into the aspirations of psychological researchers and also to shed light on some of their standard methods and day-to-day concerns. Also, since psychology is not just a laboratory exercise, I show the relationships between psychological concepts and human experiences.

Much has been left out. I have not discussed attention, one of the focal points of my research. The nature of human control structures, and the new, exciting possibility of mental mechanisms based on semi-autonomous active processing structures, "demons," are absent here. My most recent work concerns the nature of human performance: how we do skilled motor acts, the kinds of errors we make in everyday life, and the possible underlying mental structures that give rise to these errors. These are also absent from the book.

However, the direction of my recent work is suggested in the last chapter. In fact, the writing of that chapter has caused me to change my research efforts. I have become increasingly concerned with the lack of consideration for the needs of the user in the design of technological devices. This deficiency has had serious consequences. One result is alienation from modern technology. Another is the increased opportunity for error in the use of technological devices, whether they be home appliances, digital watches, or powerplants and aircraft.

We have a choice. We can either use technology to enrich our lives or allow it to degrade us. If we choose enrichment, designers will be required to take into account human needs, functions, and capabilities. However, if we do not choose this course, then the machine will not become our servant, but we will become its slave.

Many people have come to my aid during the writing of this book. I thank Ed Immergut for suggesting the project and for his continued support and encouragement. As a result of the critical but constructive guidance of a most perceptive editor, Pat Lauber, the manuscript has been through two major revisions since the first time I "finished" it. Julie Lustig has acted as my personal editorial consultant, patiently rereading my material, correcting and modifying it, and turning my illegible typing into clean manuscript. And my family has patiently put up with my peculiar working habits.

Much of the work I describe reflects my interactions with my colleagues and students in the LNR Research Group at the University of California at San Diego. I owe them many thanks. Dave Rumelhart and Don Gentner have been continual collaborators in my work. Ross Bott, Eileen Conway, Greg Haerr, Serge Larochelle, Matthew Lewis, Bob Neches, Al Stevens, Peggy Stowell, and Michael D. Williams have all contributed to the ideas and research reported here. All other members of the LNR Research Group, although not directly involved in my work, have contributed in important ways to the general spirit and philosophy that have guided me.

The research reported here was supported primarily by the Personnel and Training Research Program of the Office of Naval Research and by the Cybernetics Technology Office of the Advanced Research Projects Agency. Marshall Farr, Joe Young, and Henry Halff are responsible for the intelligent supervision of the former program, and Harry O'Neill for the latter office. Scientific progress cannot continue unless there is perceptive and flexible monetary support for research. I am grateful that we have received such support.

March 1982   *Donald A. Norman*

Learning and Memory

1

How Do We Learn?
How Do We Remember?

How do we learn? "Practice," says the piano teacher. "Practice three hours a day, every day, and in four or five years you will have made much progress." "Study," says the history professor. "Practice," says the tennis instructor or the track coach. Practice, study, practice. Whenever the task is at all complex, whether it is the acquisition of a skill such as piano playing, tennis, or juggling, the performance of sleight-of-hand tricks, or the mastery of an intellectual activity such as chess, go, mathematics, or 17th-century history—the procedure is the same: study, practice. Learning takes time; learning takes effort.

Consider how long it takes to learn a language. Children are still learning the grammar of their native language when they are well into their teenage years. The learning of vocabulary continues over the entire life span. An adult may never manage all the subtleties of a second language.

How long does it take to learn? There can be no definite answer, because there may be no end to the learning of a topic. Over the years I have watched a lot of experts. I have asked them how long they practice each day and how many years they had been learning. I have watched myself learn to juggle, to ride a unicycle (badly), to use new computer systems. Five thousand hours seems to be a reasonable minimum for learning such things. That sounds like a lot of time. It isn't. Five thousand hours is the equivalent of two and a half years of study, eight hours a day, five days a week, 50 weeks a year.

My observations of experts at table tennis, baseball, juggling and close-up magic, psychology, programming, and chess give much the same answer. Almost any activity that is difficult enough to have experts or professionals apparently requires thousands of hours of study and practice over periods of years to reach great competence.

With intellectual activities, one problem of learning is simply the size of the task. How does one learn a complex intellectual topic? Few ideas seem difficult when examined in isolation. Yet one sits, one struggles. The task is not easy. The difficulty seems to lie in the interrelationships among the ideas that must be acquired. It is the totality of the topic that requires time and mental effort.

With sports or the performing arts, there is an additional issue: the body and limbs must be controlled with great precision. This requires motor learning, an accomplishment that is both the same as, and different from, the learning of intellectual skills. Motor skills can be developed to high levels of performance. A single piano piece by Chopin may last 20 minutes and require the playing of 10,000 notes. Some piano pieces require the performer to play up to 25 notes per second for many minutes. A Russian circus performer is reported to have balanced four sticks simultaneously (one stick resting on his head, one on each hand, and one on the top of one foot), each with a ball on the top, while riding a tall "giraffe" unicycle. Practice, practice, practice. It is only by constant, prolonged training that such motor-control feats are possible.

How do we remember? Some events are easy to remember. You probably made no effort to remember what you ate at your last meal, yet if I asked you to recall that meal, you would probably do so with ease. I make no effort to remember casual conversations or the books I read or the comic strips in the newspaper. Yet I do remember them, at least for a while. Tomorrow when I read the same 20 comic strips again, I will automatically pick up the thread of each story, although each strip is different, each a fragment.

Sometimes remembrance comes only with difficulty. Learning a person's name, a telephone number, or a foreign-language vocabulary may come painfully and with great effort—or perhaps not at all. What is it that makes some things easy to learn, others hard? Why can some high-school students rattle off the statistics of sports players' performances with apparent ease, yet fail to learn (remember) topics in the classroom that actually seem to be easier? Motivation? Not always. Sometimes material that one has difficulty learning is more important and more interesting than material that is learned without effort.

To remember is to have managed three things successfully: the acquisition, retention, and retrieval of information. Failure to remember means failure at managing one of those three things.

If we store some aspects of everything we do, then there is a lot of information in memory, enough to make organization critical. The best organizational strategies involve putting the material to be learned into frameworks that naturally guide the retrieval process. That calls for "understanding," for having such a good grasp of the material to be acquired that it fits naturally into an existing framework of knowledge. The new material is understood, it fits, and with little effort it is both acquired and made retrievable.

Learning and remembering are closely related concepts. But learning is more than simply remembering; it is also performance, the ability to do a task with skill. In this book, I use the term "learning" to refer to the act of deliberate study of a specific body of material, so that the material can be retrieved at will and used with skill. Learning involves purposeful remembering and skillful performance.

In the pages that follow, I present a personal, idiosyncratic tour of selected problems in the study of learning and memory, problems that have absorbed my own efforts for a good many years. I am a psychologist interested in discovering the mechanisms of the mind. The level of description I use is that of psychology: a description of functions and properties of mechanisms of the mind. I discuss the possible structures and functions of memory, the representation and use of knowledge, and the ways in which psychological processes and knowledge combine to yield human behavior, beliefs, and understanding.

There are many possible perspectives from which to view human learning and memory. Psychological mechanisms are, of course, realized in brain structure. And human behavior does not take place in a vacuum. It is purposeful and usually interacts with the environment, with other people, and with culture and society. Human beings are biological animals, adapted through millions of years of evolutionary history. Much of human behavior—and most of the human body—is devoted to the central task of existence: regulation of body processes and maintenance of life. A complete picture of human behavior requires the different perspectives of biology, the neurosciences, anthropology, sociology, philosophy, and linguistics.

Biologists are concerned with the biological heritage of human beings. Neuroscientists might examine how chemicals influence learning and memory, or, by studying electrical recordings, attempt to trace the neurological circuits. Sociologists and anthropologists examine the role of the individual human in society, in the environment, and in a culture. Learning and memory help transmit cultural knowledge from generation to generation. Moreover, the use of human memory has changed dramatically as technological devices have extended the powers of human intellect. The invention of paper made possible the easy recording of thoughts, ideas, and speeches, thus eliminating the need for elaborate skills of memorization. The printing press, the typewriter, the tape recorder, and now the computer have further modified how and what we learn and remember and perhaps even how we think.

Each perspective also tends to contribute a different level of specification of the processes. Neuroscientists speak at the detailed level of biochemistry and electrical potentials. Others speak in more global terms of the individual human and of human interactions. I work at an intermediate level, and speak of functional mechanisms such as "perception," or "visual short-term memory." My approach is most closely related to that taken in the discipline of artificial intelligence, the major difference is the long-term goal. I wish to understand human beings, and the hypotheses of human mental mechanisms are tested through experiment and observation. For many researchers in artificial intelligence the goal is to construct intelligent machines, even if the mechanisms by which the machines work differ from those of the human. I believe this to be essential work, because by understanding the workings of intelligent machines we can better understand human mechanisms. But in this book, the emphasis is on human functioning, human capabilities, and the search for specification of the human mind.

We are all studying cognition, each of us from a different viewpoint, each at a different level of description. The science of cognition requires all of us together, each working on a different part of the structure. Cognitive scince is a new discipline, created out of the intersecting interests of philosophers, neuroscientists, sociologists, anthropologists, linguists, psychologists, and researchers in artificial intelligence. This book is about one small part of cognitive science, and it is written from the viewpoint of a psychologist.

2

Sensory Memory

Wave your hand in front of your face. The faint trace that remains after your hand is gone, a remnant of the event just past, is visible evidence of a sensory memory system. Close your hand into a fist, rapidly extend two fingers, then as quickly as possible form the fist again. If you watch closely, you will see a trace of your fingers that lasts long enough for you to count them. Move your hands parallel to each other but in opposite directions. Quickly wave them once before your eyes. Notice the subtle, indescribable feeling of motion associated with each faint trace. The feeling is real. Suppose there is flashed before you a complex image consisting of many objects, some moving clockwise in small circles, others moving counterclockwise. The image vanishes and an arrow points somewhere within the former area of the image. You will be able to report the direction in which the object in that particular place moved. The trace lasts for a few hundred milliseconds after the physical image is gone.

The fading trace of a briefly exposed visual signal has long interested psychologists. In the mid-1800s the question asked was: How many objects can the mind apprehend at one time? (The modern psychologist asks: Is the number of objects reported a result of immediate apprehension or is it a report from the fading memory trace of what has been perceived?) The task of answering the question was approached in various ways, starting with the simple act of throwing a handful of objects on the ground and noting how many could be seen clearly when they were all momentarily stopped by hit-

Visual Sensory Memory

Take a flashlight, point it at your head, turn it on, and rotate your hand in a circle. Note that the light can be seen lagging behind the flashlight. Rotate your hand at a rate that just causes the trailing light to form a circle. Now, get a friend to time your actions. Maintain the rate of rotation while you count the number of circles you make in ten seconds. Divide the number by 10, take the reciprocal, and you have the number of seconds the image from each circle stays usable. This is a crude (but surprisingly accurate) method of estimating the duration of visual sensory memory.

Try the same experiment with bright or dim lights, in a brightly lighted room, in the dark, or in these other ways:

In the dark with dark-adapted eyes (after 30 minutes in the dark).

With central vision, looking straight at the light so that it is seen by the color sensitive part of the eye (the cones in the fovea).

Looking away, seeing the light from the corner of the eye, in order to use only the part of the eye that is sensitive to black and white (the rods in the periphery).

The results will differ.

Sensory stores are commonly thought to be of use in watching motion pictures or television, where the discrete flickering images are perceived as continuous ones. Sensory stores also play an impor-

ting the ground. "You can easily make the experiment for yourselves," said Sir William Hamilton in the mid-1800s, "but you must beware of grouping the objects into classes. If you throw a handful of marbles on the floor, you will find it difficult to view at once more than six, or seven at most, without confusion; but if you group them into twos, or threes, or fives, you can comprehend as many units; because the mind considers these groups only as units."

The experiment is crude, yet more modern, more elaborate experiments provide the same conclusions. Consider the observation about "grouping," a most important comment. Grouping, or organization, the changing of what might otherwise be many independent units into a smaller number of organized groups of units, is one of the features of human perception and memory. Such features form the basis of current studies.

It took the invention of the tachistoscope in the 1880s to give proper contant role in reading and in perceiving in general. They are useful for such tasks as walking at night down a dark trail where rapid waving of a flashlight allows illumination of a region that is wider than the beam of the light itself; your visual sensory store maintains the image of the illuminated portion while you take the next step or two.

Amateur artists and cartoonists often indicate motion with a receding trail of images behind the speeding object. Is this just an abstract convention or does it have its origins in the fading trace within the sensory store? We do indeed see fast moving objects with a trail behind. The trail of a meteor is a streak of light; our image of the thrown ball outlives the passage time. Is this convention or a mirroring of subjective reality?

trol to the "fading-trace" experiment. The tachistoscope is a device that presents one of several visual fields to an observer for closely specified durations and permits precise control over the positioning, illumination, and contrast of the images. The first tachistoscopes were mechanical; today they may incorporate half-silvered mirrors and electronically controlled gas-discharge tubes as illumination sources. Tachistoscopes with television and oscilloscope displays (with computer control of the image that is to be presented) are the most sophisticated, but they receive less use than one might suppose, because they are often less precise in the control of light levels and in the range of visual material that can be presented than their electrical-optical-mechanical counterparts.

In any event, more can be seen at once than can be reported. The fading memory trace that lags behind a visual image allows the processing to continue for a duration exceeding that of the image itself. When an experimenter tests a person's knowledge of an image by selectively asking about parts of the image pointed to by a probe that comes on at controlled periods prior to, during, and following the image, the experimenter can deduce something about the nature of the memory trace. It can be described as a decaying exponential; the clarity of the memory trace decreases with a time constant between 100 and 150 milliseconds, see Figure 2-1. (A time constant of 100 milliseconds means that each 100 milliseconds, the image decreases in clarity to about one-third of its previous value.)

The evidence is strong that there is a visual sensory memory that retains rather detailed information about a visual image for as long as several seconds. This relatively long duration is a result of the phenomenal dynamic range of the visual system—the intensity of the strongest signal that can be processed without pain or significant distortion is about 10^{10} times the intensity of the weakest signal that can be detected. It takes about 25 time con-

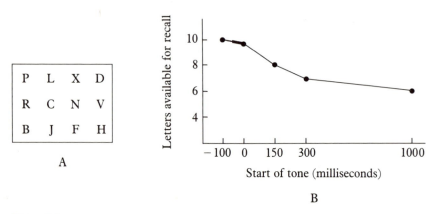

Figure 2-1.
In this experiment a person looked into the tachistoscope, and stared at a dimly illuminated "fixation cross." When ready, the person pushed a button, and 0.5 second later, a display of 9 or 12 randomly selected consonants (A) was shown for exactly 50 milliseconds (indicated by heavy bar in part B). The person was required to report letters from the row indicated by a tone: A high frequency tone signalled the top row of 4 consonants, a middle frequency tone signalled the middle row, and a low frequency tone signalled the bottom row. The tone was presented at different times: 50 milliseconds before the consonants, simultaneously with the consonants, and 150, 300, 500, and 1,000 milliseconds after the consonants. Because people do about equally well on each row, we assume that the total number of letters available is three times the fraction correctly reported from the row signalled by the tone. (If asked to recall the entire display, people do not do well, in part because recall of the first few items interferes with the ability to recall the rest. This technique minimizes interference.) [Experiment and data by Sperling (1960).]

stants for the perceived signal level to decay over that range, or about 2 to 3 seconds.

Why do we have such a system? Several explanations are plausible. The system allows maintenance of the visual image during an eye blink. The memory may be essential for pattern recognition, allowing visual signals to stay around for some useful amount of time. Then again, we may have the system by an accident of design. It could be a by-product of the eye's mechanisms, such as after-traces of optical-chemical reactions on the retina. I don't adhere to this last view. The entire body is exquisitely constructed; nonfunctional aspects are not to be expected. My belief is that visual memory serves the later stages of processing by maintaining an image for a sufficient length of time to let those stages do their jobs. Complete evidence has yet to be gathered, so a final determination cannot be made.

The story is actually much more complex than this brief account suggests. There is still active debate concerning the mechanisms responsible for visual sensory memory; as for the other senses, several experiments have demonstrated that similar memory systems exist for the auditory and tactile systems. But for current purposes, it is enough to know that such memory systems do exist and to know something of their nature.

Sensory memory is the natural place to begin this story of learning and memory. The goal is the uncovering of all the forms of memory and their use, function, and the forms of knowledge within them. The study of visual sensory memory gives a hint of the techniques helpful at the start of the exploration, as well as some of the problems one encounters. Now it is time to follow the trail onward, deeper into the stages of human information processing.

3

Stages of Processing

Say aloud the numbers 1, 7, 4, 2, 8. Next, without looking back, repeat them. Try again if you must, perhaps closing your eyes, the better to "hear" the sound still echoing in mental activity. Have someone read a random sentence to you. What were the words? The memory of the just present is available immediately, clear and complete, without apparent mental effort.

What did you eat for dinner three days ago? Now the feeling differs. It takes time to recover the answer, which is neither as clear nor as complete a remembrance as that of the just present, and the recovery is likely to require considerable mental effort. Retrieval of the past differs from retrieval of the just present. More effort is required, less clarity results. Indeed, the "past" need not be so long ago. Without looking back, what were those digits? For some people, this retrieval now takes time and effort.

The distinction between the availability of memory of the just present and memory of the past so impressed the American philosopher and psychologist William James that in 1890 he proposed that two different mechanisms, or processes, were responsible. The first, which allows effortless retrieval of the just present, he called primary memory; the second, which requires effort and search, he called secondary memory. The distinction continues to be a useful one.

The psychological present is a duration, not an instant. Our conscious awareness of the just present is measurable. The last words of a spoken sentence, the last few sounds of a ticking clock, the sequence of an event, such as throwing a ball at a wall and observing it hit and bounce away—these are the contents of our immediate perception. When someone speaks to you while you are engrossed in reading or thinking, you are likely to ask, "What did you say?" But often before the other person can reply, you manage to recover the words yourself from the primary-memory structure that has kept them available.

Ask for the recall of a sentence spoken minutes or hours ago and retrieval is of a different nature. Recovery of events of the past requires considerable work (if indeed retrieval can be accomplished at all): search, reconstruction, effort—and even then, after the expenditure of considerable time and mental energy, what is reconstructed may contain only the gist of what happened. As laboratory studies of the testimony of eyewitnesses have shown, memory of the past cannot be trusted; the apparent vividness and richness of a memory of an accident or a crime may be misleading. But memory of the just present differs considerably from memory of the past. Memory of the present brings with it memory of the sensory details that accompany the information. It is a memory that is detailed, complete, and reasonably accurate in its content. Moreover, the information is easily available. No search is required because the information is there, readily accessible to consciousness.

Sensory memory is at the periphery of processing; it is one of the first stages through which information passes. We cannot exert much control over the processing that takes place in sensory memory. We can close our eyes or turn our heads, but the signals that impinge on our eyes and ears arrive at their respective memories regardless of our thoughts and desires. The first classification of the signals, identifying their meaningful mental referents, takes place soon after, and the result is made available for conscious awareness within primary and secondary memory. It is within primary memory that we first have conscious control over the processing of information. That first control is slight: we can choose what to do with material in primary memory, but we cannot control what gets there. Nonetheless, it is at this point that mental strategies start playing a major role in the processing. We can selectively attend to material within primary memory, go over it, follow its implications, interrelate it with other knowledge available from secondary memory. Sometimes we must search secondary memory for that information. The search process involves many mechanisms and control processes that give flexibility and power to the use of memory.

Deeper in the memory system, things become more difficult to pin down. Strategies and processes interact with knowledge. Do you know the product of 3 times 4? You probably have that stored away. But what about 479 times 3648? You don't have the answer on the tip of your tongue, but you do know how to find out. Not everything is stored. We sometimes derive what we need to know; thought can substitute for knowledge. The structure of memory becomes less important than what one does with the knowledge in terms of organization, interpretation, elaboration, and understanding.

Figure 3-1 illustrates what might be called "the conventional view" of the sequence of processing stages. This view is currently under attack, with various authorities (myself for one) arguing that these simple sequential sets are not adequate to do the assigned task because there must be so much interconnection and cross-communication that the concept of individual stages, each in its own neatly labeled box, loses cohesion and sensibleness. Nonetheless, these stages are a good first approximation of the workings of the memory system.

We have no conscious control over many perceptions. Normally, if a tree is in front of our open eyes, we have no way to avoid seeing it once the image falls on the retina. It is possible, of course, to deny that the tree is there, but as the signals flow from the retina through the psychological mechanisms of pattern recognition, there is no control over the processing. In abnormal situations—hypnosis, hallucination, or Freudian repression—a person may deny seeing the tree, but the truth is that the tree is seen, even if the viewer honestly denies knowledge of the sight.

Psychology seems to be the self-obvious science, because we are all aware of what goes on inside the mind—or are we? I look at the world and I see what is there. I think back to an event of the past and re-create it in my thoughts. But who is this "I" that is doing the seeing or the remembering? Look again at the drawing of processing stages. Where is the central "I" of conscious existence? Consciousness is not well understood. It is only beginning to be studied scientifically. Consciousness is not the topic of this book, but it will hover over us, an essential piece of the puzzle left out.

What is known to each of us through consciousness is only a part of what actually takes place in our minds. Sometimes our conscious impressions are

---

Figure 3-1.
This diagram of the stages of the human information processing system is a combination of the conventional and modern views. To simplify matters, the input and output processes are shown divorced from one another, despite the well known interrelationships between them. Input and output are shown interacting through the memory system, again a simplification. The layout of the six clouds floating above memory is not significant. The purpose is to emphasize that these processes and functions are all a part of higher mental functioning, but the mechanisms are unknown. This diagram is best viewed as a reminder of the various kinds of functions and interactions of the information processing mechanisms, not as a schematic circuit diagram.[From D. A. Norman, ed., Perspectives in Cognitive Science, *1981. Reprinted by permission of the publisher, Lawrence Erlbaum Associates, Inc., Hillsdale, New Jersey, and Ablex Publishing Co., Norwood, New Jersey.]*

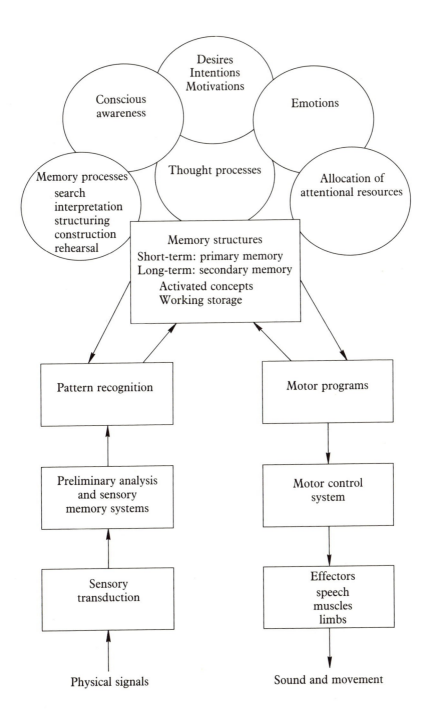

simply incomplete, sometimes they are quite erroneous. Subconscious mechanisms are of critical importance. And, like employees protective of their top management, subconscious mechanisms can block conscious access to events (as with the inability, induced by hypnosis, to "see" a tree, or as with the distortion of reality caused by mental ailments).

Conscious awareness is limited in all aspects of seeing, hearing, perception, memory, thought, emotion, and action. There is a simple demonstration of this. You may believe you control your actions, but in fact you have control only at the highest level of intention. You cannot and do not monitor each muscle of the body. Clench your hand into a fist, thumb on top of the fingers—you are not aware of the muscle control, only of the intention and the result. When you closed your fingers to make the fist, did the thumb initiate its movement before or after the fingers moved? It is likely that you can answer only if you observed your own actions. Note how automatically the parts of the body move. If the thumb happens to be in the way of making a fist, it moves smoothly aside, lets the fingers clench, and then goes back on top, all without the need for conscious guidance or even awareness.

Conscious control starts somewhere in primary memory, where one can deliberately attend to or ignore information that has arrived. Rehearsal, the psychologist's term for the deliberate act of repeating the material that is in primary memory, is a conscious control mechanism that allows the material to stay within primary memory for longer than it otherwise would. Deliberate processing occurs in primary memory as an aid to remembering, interpreting, or following the implications of arriving information.

We rehearse the phrase we have just heard or the one we are about to say. We rehearse a person's name when we first hear it. We rehearse the movements we will make if we are about to throw a dart or perform an intricate operation. We rehearse the body motions just performed on a demanding ski run. We mentally simulate the motions of doing. Mental simulation may even weakly evoke the proper muscle controls. If rehearsers are surrounded with loud noise, they can be seen mumbling. Musicians can sometimes be seen moving their fingers slightly. Skiers can be seen making subtle body movements. The division between thought and action seems slight in these cases.

Within primary memory we can choose what we wish to do with information. We can select or ignore, follow one direction or another. Most important, we can choose to think of the implications of past experience and relate what is happening to what has happened. We can try to predict future events, or we can ignore one thing to concentrate on another. What we do with the information within primary memory has profound effects on our ability to get at it later on and to use it for some other purpose. The depth and type of processing within primary memory are of critical importance.

Even these early stages of processing are far from simple. All is not as it seems. There is a clear conceptual difference between our knowledge of the

On the Person in the Head

The description of the use of memory processes has a peculiar flavor to it. It sounds as if the memory system were something like a friend of whom we could ask a question and who might work without our knowing it for days, surprising us with the result. What does it mean to talk of the memory system's telling us something? To whom is the memory system reporting?

When I say I know that I know something, who is the I that does the knowing and how can this I be separate from the part of me that has the knowledge? And what can this quote mean: ". . . a process that we thought we had terminated keeps functioning and suddenly reports some result and diverts our attention. . . ." Reports some result? To whom? From whom? Isn't all of this taking place within the same person, the same head, the same mind?

The language I have used is deliberately suggestive of a mental organization in which the I, or ego, is identified with conscious control and awareness, and the control and awareness are limited in scope. The basic notion is that there are different levels of activity going on within the mind and that only some of these are under direct voluntary control; only some produce results of which one is consciously aware.

Thus the memory system is viewed as being separate from the consciousness system, available for use, but requiring active search and examination of its contents to get at the parts that are useful. Both conscious and subconscious processing play important roles. The psychology of consciousness is in its infancy, and little is known about the nature of systems that have self-awareness or consciousness. This happens to be a topic of particular interest to me, and although I do not discuss the issues in depth in this book, the language has been deliberately selected to reflect a separation between processes. Thus when I speak of "initiating a search of memory," the initiator is the consciousness system. When I speak of being surprised by some thought, I mean to indicate that the subconscious processes have pursued a line of reasoning, followed trails within the memory system, and reached some result which then becomes known by the consciousness system. The consciousness system might very well be unaware of the fact that any thought was taking place at all, and the surprise can result both from the nature of the information being reported and from the fact that the information appeared at that particular time.

present and of the past. We are aware of the present, whereas the past must be sought. Our awareness of the present is immediate and direct, but much of its clarity results from considerable processing and enrichment of the incoming sensory signals.

Examine the visual world around you—it seems clear, distinct, colorful. Yet these qualities are created by your mind out of fragmentary, incomplete information. The only part of your visual field that is truly distinct, with complete information about color, is the part that comes from the fovea— the central part of the retina. This area is small—about five degrees of visual angle—barely big enough to encompass three letters of this text when seen from a normal reading distance. Information from the rest of the eye is of a different quality. There is a neural organization on the retina that transforms an image, enhances its contours, is sensitive to motion, and changes the signals from the three different color receptors into balanced pairs of opposing processes: red versus green, blue versus yellow, and light versus dark. The organization changes from the center to the periphery of the retina because few color receptors exist outside the fovea. In addition, there is a sharp vertical division in the visual field: all neural information from the right half of each eye is sent to the right half of the brain and all neural information from the left half of each eye is sent to the left half of the brain. I have long searched for some sign of that line in my perception. Shouldn't there be a vertical line? Perhaps the colors of the left half shouldn't quite match those of the right. But the visual perception I experience shows no signs of the peculiar nature of retinal and brain processing. The whole world appears clear, distinct, in color. And when I move my eyes or body, the world remains stationary. (But if I push my eyeball with my finger, the world seems to move, a clue to the intricate mechanisms that update my internal model of the world and that must determine whether a moving image on the retina results from a moving object in the world or from the movement of the eyes while the world is stationary. And what if both the objects and the eyes are moving? Such are the questions that motivate the psychologist.)

Complete interpretation and understanding of arriving signals require more than is contained in the signals themselves. Often the arriving information is incomplete or ambiguous. The total percept must be fleshed out with conceptualizations that can be provided only by the cognitive system's actively devising internal structures within which to interpret the new information. The part of the analysis that proceeds from the higher conceptual levels is called "conceptually guided processing," or sometimes "top-down processing." The part of the analysis that proceeds up from the sensory data, extracting relevant features and piecing together the informative unit that the data must represent, is called "data-driven processing," or sometimes "bottom-up processing." Both types are needed for full analysis of the signals.

Conceptually guided processing seems to require use of the limited pool of conscious resources that are available for mental activity. Moreover, conceptually guided processes seem to be controllable, subject to our intentions and desires. Data-driven processing is apparently more automatic, less under any active control, and probably does not require any resources that might be involved in general cognitive activity. The point is that full analysis and understanding require the combination of a multitude of efforts, some automatic, some not. Conscious experiences are interpreted experiences. Some information never becomes conscious, thus providing a means of shielding ourselves from the massive quantity of sensory data that impinge on the neural receptors. Some information is fabricated especially for consciousness, as when a past experience is reconstructed by the memory system in a manner not always consistent with the original. And some information is suppressed, perhaps as a means of shielding ourselves from knowledge that one part of us thinks is dangerous or unsettling to other parts of us.

As a psychologist, I want to know how the mind works. What are the mechanisms of mind, the procedures, the knowledge structures? But I have a problem: I cannot have direct access to another person's mind, and I have learned not to trust all that seems to be accessible in my own. I am left, therefore, with the need for careful observation, deduction, theorizing, and experimentation. With the aid of experiments I can observe how people respond, what they can remember, and how they learn. With the aid of appropriate theories, I can focus my questions, design my experiments, and interpret my observations.

Primary Memory

Say a sentence and ask someone to repeat it out loud. What is recovered and what is not tells something about the nature of the memory structure. This simple experiment suggests a basic paradigm for experimental investigations. But if the experiment is so simple, why do psychologists make such a fuss about these things?

To begin with, the experiment is flawed. I may sit here with my own private notions of what our memory systems are like, but my private notions, derived from a lifelong knowledge of my own actions and capabilities, may be faulty. To find out how memory systems work I need some objectivity. Yet I can't get access to your memory. I can't touch it, measure it, or record from it directly. I do, however, have access to your eyes, your ears, your behavior—what you say and what you do. I can give you a sentence to remember, and how well you do may depend on the ability of your perceptual system to comprehend the sentence, on your ability to concentrate, on the knowledge structures you bring to bear from past learning, on your interest in helping me, and, to some small extent, on the properties of your immediate memory system that are my goal to discover.

Consider the following sentence:

the name of this book is not how the mind works

That is a simple sentence: 11 words, 37 letters. You should have no trouble repeating it. How large a memory does it take to remember the sentence? Is the sentence made up of 1, 11, or 37 items? The answer depends on the choice of unit. Here is another test of memory. Try repeating this set of words:

works mind the how not is book this of name the

Same words, reverse order. Memory isn't as good. Of course, you might be able to remember the forward order and then run it backward when asked for a recall. In that case I would discover not what your real memory capacity is, but rather how clever you are at rederiving the required information. The difficulty is even more general: How do I know whether you actually remembered the first sentence or just kept the gist and reconstructed the words when required?

I can continue and arrange the letters in random order. Here are the 37 letters in the sentence, more than you can handle:

n s b w a e e o t f t o i o t e h r h w n i k
o d t i n h m o s m o k s h

My point is that the memory system does not store things in simple cubicles. How much you can remember depends on how well you can interpret what you are remembering. My measures are contaminated by many factors. The mind insists on finding meaning and patterns, and then using them to help recover and reconstruct what it attempts to remember. Person A tells you that her telephone number is 345-6789. Person B tells you that his number is 749-3658. The same 7 digits occur but are arranged in a different order. The first number is easy to remember, the second is hard. Why? The first number can be interpreted as "an ascending sequence starting with 3."

When there is an interpretation, the memory system works better. We are designed to be understanders. There is an old illustration along these lines. Try to remember the sequence

9162536496481

By itself, the task is hard—13 digits is a bit more than the average person can keep in mind for long. Now think of the numbers in the sequence as squares: $3^2 = 9$, $4^2 = 16$, $\cdots$, $9^2 = 81$. This time "memory" comes easily. But is it memory or is it reconstruction? This basic question plagues students of memory. Why should there be any difference? Memory is reconstructive. The memory system makes use of all the power it can. It takes as much information as it can retrieve and puts the pieces together with the aid of knowledge of such situations, of constraints, and of the world at large.

How does one test memory alone when each part of the system aids the rest? The answer is to try to isolate it in order to control the effect of meaning, and thereby perhaps control the amount of reconstruction that takes place. That is why psychologists turn to nonsense words or randomly arranged digits (taking care that the random arrangement does not produce a "meaningful" sequence). We find some willing people—experimental subjects—and subject them to memory tests: "Here is a sequence of randomly arranged one-syllable words; report back as many as you can." The classic results are shown in Figure 4-1.

A suspicion of what is happening comes from being a subject and observing the experiment. The words arrive, one every second. You rehearse them, saying them over and over to yourself, the better to keep them around where you can get hold of them. You may try to form connections among words, ". . . home . . . crowd . . . store. . . ." Any association, any image, anything. There isn't always time because the next word comes and then the

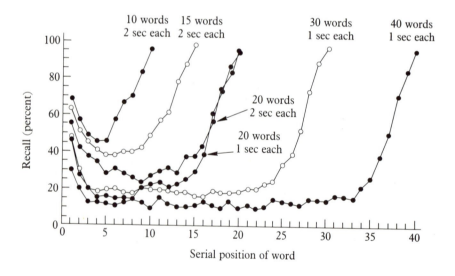

Figure 4-1.
These classic serial position curves show the results of an experiment. Consider the curve labelled "30 words, 1 second each." A list of 30 unrelated monosyllabic words was read to a group of people, at a rate of one word per second. As soon as the last word had been read, they were requested to write down all they could remember, in any order. This procedure is called free recall. The graph shows the relative frequency with which each word was recalled as a function of its serial position: the position it occupied in the original reading of the list. [Experiment by B. B. Murdock, Jr. Graph from Lindsay and Norman (1977).]

next. The list finally ends, and you are supposed to recall as much of it as you can. The last few words are clear, distinct, and readily available. They seem to be in an "echo box." Quick, say them. Alas, the act of pronouncing one of the words weakens the memory of the others. Each time you say something, the echoes become even weaker. Memory for the rest of the list is more stable, what little there is. Only the last part of the list seems to reside in a fragile temporary state, the echo box. But the items in the echo box are easy to retrieve. These introspections correspond to our theory that the last few words in the list are still in primary memory, where they are available as part of the record of the present. The theory is buttressed by the fact that a delay filled with mind-occupying trivia (such as counting backward by threes or crossing out letters on a piece of paper) causes the material in the echo box to disappear but leaves all the rest of the list relatively intact (Figure 4-2).

At this point the studies on primary memory proliferate. There are a lot of questions to be asked. Can we get a "pure" measure of primary memory? I tried once. I gave subjects a list of digits to learn and later probed for a specific position in the list. The project was laborious and time-consuming. If you want to test 10 different positions in a list and if you want to get 100 observations of the memory ability at each point, that's 1000 lists to be learned. Given a presentation rate of one item per second and allowing time for responding and a short recovery period before each list, that's 5½ hours of listening to lists. Two hours a day is about as long as a person can do this, and so it will take four days to finish, allowing for starting and stopping, for rest breaks, and for practice trials at the start of each day to get the person back into the swing of the experiment. And that's just to study one person, under one condition.

Another question: Does information in primary memory dissipate as a result of the passage of time or because of interference from other items and operations? It is surprisingly difficult to tell. The earliest evidence favored time decay, the later evidence (including my own, I thought) favored decay as a result of interference. But other experimenters reanalyzed my data and collected their own; they showed that both time and interference seem to be important. The time decay seems to take place with a time constant of about 10 to 15 seconds; interference effects have an "item" constant of 3 or 4 items. One important finding is that when people are attempting to recall visually presented words and letters, the errors they make are phonological. Present the word *nail* visually and a few seconds later it is apt to be written as *male*. Present the letter E visually, and it is apt to be written as G or perhaps V, almost never as F (which would be a nice example of visual confusion). Evidently the visual information is recoded auditorily in primary memory, at least when the items to be recalled are words or letters.

Primary memory presents psychologists with a number of puzzles. Is pri-

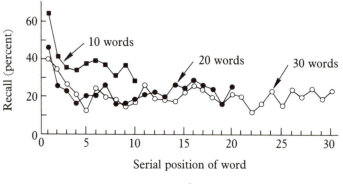

A

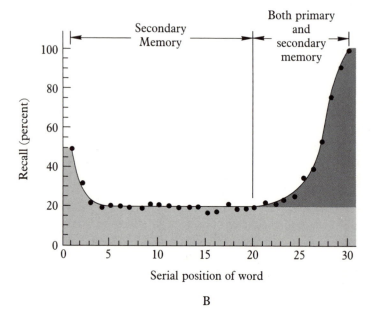

B

Figure 4-2.
When a free recall experiment is performed, but with a delay between the end of the list and the time when recall is allowed, the results are shown by the curves shown in part A: the last part of the curve is flattened out. In this experiment by Postman and Phillips (1965), when the last word in the list had been presented, the experimental subjects were required to count backward by threes for 20 seconds (e.g., 942, 939, 936, . . .). The usual interpretation is that the counting interfered with those words that were retained only in primary memory as indicated in part B, which shows one of the curves from the free recall experiment reported on page 20. [Graphs from Lindsay and Norman (1977).]

mary memory also working memory, the place where partial results of problem solving and thinking activity reside? Is primary memory a place or a process? Is it a separate mechanism within the head that gets, holds, and transmits information? Or is it perhaps the result of normal processing activity, so that certain information within mental structures temporarily receives a special status, is possibly "activated" so that it can be readily retrieved and used?

Does it make any difference whether primary memory is a place or a structure or whether it is a process such as activation? In terms of the functional properties of memory, there may be no difference whatsoever. In terms of the possible physiological mechanisms of the brain, there is a major difference. The difference might also be revealed by the kinds of abnormalities of memory that can occur or in the disruptions of memory by other activity or accidental trauma. There are other differences as well. Viewing memory as an activation suggests that the capacity of primary memory is related to the problem of discriminating activated items from those that are not activated. Does activation decay with time? Does each activated item require some sort of reactivation process to be kept active? Does the activation level decrease as more items become activated? All these questions are somewhat different from those one might ask if primary memory were considered as a structure. With a structure, the capacity of the memory is the size of the structure; capacity has no bearing on the ability to discriminate.

The difficulties in studying primary memory are simple compared with those in studying secondary memory. With a large memory system, organization is a key factor in its use. Secondary memory is immense, its boundaries not yet established. It maintains the experiences of a lifetime. And so in my discussion of secondary memory, the emphasis will shift to the problems of organization and of retrieval, of finding what one seeks. A second emphasis will be on representation. How is information represented so that it can be used to make inferences, to answer questions, to guide the thought processes?

The major issues in secondary memory have to do with the organization and structure of the knowledge contained within it. Hence the problem of studying secondary memory becomes individualized, because each person maintains a unique record of experiences, organized in idiosyncratic ways. The structures of secondary memory and the principles of their use are common to all people. But the knowledge contained within secondary memory and the organization of such knowledge must differ for each person, as an anecdote concerning my own wanderings through secondary memory clearly demonstrates.

5

Secondary Memory

When we first moved into our new home, I installed a smoke detector. After some months the battery ran down, and a replacement proved difficult to find.

At about the same time, I set out to buy more photographic slide trays. I went to the nearest photography stores, but they didn't have the correct type for my projector. I tried a department store and several other stores with no success. I tried (and failed) to recollect where I had bought new trays a few years earlier.

Sometime later, I arrived in Champaign, Illinois, for a meeting and went directly to a party welcoming the participants. The next morning, as I showered in my hotel, I thought about the party and the attractive house in which it had been held. I reviewed the house mentally, recalling the smoke detector I had seen on one of the walls. A small light served as an indicator. I decided that the detector was probably plugged into the house wiring and that the light indicated the power was on.

My recollection of this electrically operated smoke detector led me to think of the battery operated detector in my own house. I wondered idly whether we should change ours to one that plugged into the house current.

That thought reminded me of the difficulty I had encountered in replacing the battery. I had finally sent to New York for one. This thought, in turn, led me to recall that when I had later visited a department store near the university where I teach, I discovered that it sold the special battery. I wandered mentally through the store and triggered the recollection that it was there that I had earlier found the right slide trays for my slide projector. (And, indeed, when I returned to San Diego I was able to purchase the trays.)

How did my thoughts in the shower in Champaign lead to a memory that had completely eluded me in San Diego?

A major difference between the retrieval failure in San Diego and the success in Champaign was the starting point. In the unsuccessful attempt I started with trays and tried to retrieve a store name. In the successful attempt I started with a store and retrieved the items it sold. Memory mechanisms work their ways differently when they are started differently. We follow trails, links, and pathways of knowledge, and where we start is critical (Figure 5-1).

The human memory is marvelous. Its powers and its foibles are overwhelming. A major property of memory is the tendency to form links, or relationships, among items. These associations seem to lie at the heart of our memory abilities. They allow us to relate our different experiences, to discover similarities, to use past experience as a basis for interpreting the present. They aid the power of creative thought—and also distract from concentrated thought. As we wander through the web of associated memories, each item we come to tempts us with distractions. To pursue logical thinking requires mental blinders, the better to ignore the lure of fond memories and to let one plunge straight through to the goal. Most of us cannot avoid distractions, sometimes to our great benefit, more often to no useful purpose.

Dangers too lurk within the paths of memory—traps, force fields, attracting us to reminiscences we might prefer to forget. Call them the trap of the green hippopotamus (for the next 10 seconds do not think of a green hippopotamus. Or better: stop and think of an emotional event of recent occurrence that was either positive or negative for you. Reflect on it for 30 seconds. This event is now your personal green hippopotamus).

Memory structures are not simply links. They are active paths, with hills and brambles, magnets and highways.

My task as a theoretical psychologist is to understand the mechanics of the memory system. But how does one explain poetic vision, wandering thought, colorful ideas? How can one collect scientific data from the multiple happenings of mental activity in which each person has private thoughts, private knowledge? Through experimental probing the experimental psychologist can reveal only a glimmer of the workings of the mind.

Freud tried to deal with some aspects of human thought, but his attempt was flawed. I suspect Freud's theories are more correct than contemporary cognitive psychologists acknowledge (in modern scientific psychology Freud is completely ignored). I also suspect that his theories are much less correct than workers in contemporary psychoanalytic theory would have us believe.

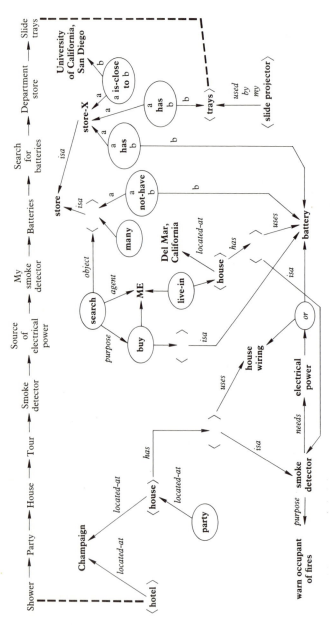

Figure 5-1. This partial, simplified representation of the contents of my memory shows the links that allowed my thoughts to wander from the shower in Champaign, Illinois, to the store at which I could buy slide trays in San Diego, California. The line of text at the top of the figure summarizes the train of thoughts. The memory structure is shown in the notation that will be explained later, in the chapter titled Semantic Networks. To understand the diagram, simply trace out the critical path, which, when translated from the diagram into pseudo-English is as follows (follow the path on the diagram). The words in boldface are nodes on the diagram; the words in italics are relations between nodes.

Start at the **hotel**, *located-at* **Champaign**. This is (obviously) related to the **party**, *located-at* a **house** (which is itself *located-at* **Champaign**). The **house** *has* in it something that *isa* **smoke detector**. The **smoke detector** *needs* **electrical power**, either from the **house wiring** *or* from **batteries**. I (**Me**, in the diagram) **searched** many **stores** for the *purpose* of **buying** batteries for a smoke detector. One of those stores (**store-X** on the diagram) *has* in it batteries for the smoke detector, and lo and behold, my memory structure also reveals that it *has* in it **trays** that are *used* by my **slide projector**.

Freud understood the nature of associations, in particular, the nature of the trap of the green hippopotamus, but he failed to provide psychologically plausible mechanisms. More important, he failed to provide a theory that could be compared with data, a theory that could be verified or that could be modified as critical results were observed. As you will see, Freud's problems have their parallel in contemporary theorizing as well—in the attempt to uncover the processing that must occur for the recovery of material stored in memory.

We usually are able to find the information we seek, we usually can answer the questions asked of us. We can learn from the relative ease of answering questions. Some things are easy to retrieve, others take a long time. It is intriguing that we are sometimes quick to know what it is we do not know, and that despite the idiosyncratic nature of secondary memory we are equally quick to agree on the relative ease or difficulty of answering various types of questions.

6

Answering Questions

What was the telephone number of the composer Ludwig van Beethoven?

As you entered the front door of the house you lived in three houses ago, was the doorknob on the left or the right?

Those two questions are favorites of mine. Most people are much faster at answering the first. There is a feeling of immediate recognition that the answer is not known and never was known, followed quickly by the realization that there is no answer—the telephone was invented after Beethoven's death. With the second question, the feeling is that the answer was once readily available, but that now it is either forgotten or, if still present, is bound to take a lot of effort to get to, more effort than the result seems to be worth.

Your reactions to the questions reveal knowledge about the contents and workings of the memory system, knowledge about knowledge, or meta-knowledge. Note that the knowledge of your lack of knowledge of Beethoven's telephone number comes rapidly, and it is likely that your introspections reflect what happened after the memory system reported the absence of information.

When we psychologists examine questions of this form, we are studying secondary memory—the human knowledge system. We need to know how information is represented, how it is retrieved, how it is used. We must ask about mental strategies and procedures. Sensory memory is automatic—there is little or nothing that affects its operations. Primary memory allows for a little control, especially for rehearsal and for selective retention and elaboration of the contents. Secondary memory also has its mixture. On the one hand, we can start and stop processes or go off and look for things here or there, using what we find to direct the search to some other spot in memory. On the other hand, when we retrieve from one spot in memory, we may trigger some interesting things, and off we go, following that line of thought, even if it is irrelevant to the original question we were following. Sometimes a process we thought we had terminated keeps functioning and suddenly reports some result that diverts our attention once again.

Simple questions often shed light on mental strategies and procedures. Consider *mgdptzy*. What does it mean? As a word it is nonsense, and its rejection is immediate. *Mgdptzy* cannot be pronounced, it does not fit the rules of orthography, and it has no meaning. The example is trivial, but the point is not. With such a peculiar combination of letters it is impossible to start the search of memory—there is no way to begin. This is an important datum. Before a search of memory can be performed, the query must be put into the form proper for the type of information sought.

Note the ease with which we all decide whether or not we know something. Even combinations of letters that look like English words (but aren't)—*mantiness* or *tralidity*—seem to be rejected immediately. How? According to some simple schemes of memory we would need to examine all the words that are known to see that these were not among them. That doesn't seem practicable, but how else could we do the job? The only answer seems to be that we have a content-addressable storage system—a system in which the route that must be taken to find the relevant information is given by the information itself. We look where "mantiness" ought to be and find nothing there.

Consider the series:

pt&*z	Not the correct symbols for a word.
mgdptzy	Correct symbols, but not a legitimate spelling.
mantiness	Legitimate word form, but no meaning is stored.
mansuetude	Legitimate word form and an actual word, but most people have never encountered it.
happiness	Legitimate word, meanings can be retrieved.

If I were to do an experiment along these lines, I would have to control for all the possible contaminants. Each query would have to be carefully presented, items randomized to avoid problems with ordering, and many different examples of each query tested to avoid accidents of peculiar letter combinations or peculiar associations. Different people would have to be presented with different orderings of items to avoid contamination from learning or boredom or other irrelevant effects. Although the experiment has not yet been done, I don't really have much doubt about its outcome. I feel certain I would find that the amount of time taken to respond to *pt &*z* would be the shortest, that *mantiness* and *mansuetude* would take the most time, and that the positive response to *happiness* would occur more quickly than responses to the prior two items.

Here is a different set of examples. The basic paradigm for this memory query is a search for a telephone number, and the mental operations that ensue depend critically on what number is being sought. (Try the task yourself as you read it, timing how long it takes to come up with the answers—if you know any.)

Query: As fast as possible, give the telephone number of each of the following:

Charles Dickens (the novelist)

the White House

your favorite local restaurant

the local fire department

your telephone of five years ago (or two telephones ago)

a friend

your current home telephone

As before, the queries take different amounts of time to be answered or rejected. Is the input a name or a place? Might it logically have a telephone? Is there any reason to suppose that you might know the number? Different amounts of information from memory are involved in each query.

Again, I expect the middle items to take the longest. "Charles Dickens" should be rejected immediately. The time for the next three items will depend on how frequently you have been exposed to them. They could take several minutes. To recall the telephone number you had five years or two telephones ago requires the prior step of determining where you lived then. Considerable effort could be required for the next step—retrieval—despite the fact that this is a number you presumably once knew well.

The two different examples of memory retrieval—identifying words and remembering telephone numbers—demonstrate some of the varied properties of memory.

In reading and listening, we can usually interpret each word within tenths of a second of its arrival at the sensory system. The recognition and retrieval of linguistic information—part of speech, tense, number, meaning, and so on—happens so rapidly that we are usually quite unaware of its operation. It is only by throwing in the very rare word or the fake word or nonsensical characters that psychologists can get some glimmer of the complexity of the operations that must be taking place. For normal words, going from sound or sight to recognition and retrieval of meaning is a fast, smooth, effortless process.

The situation changes with the converse operation: going from meaning to item. Access is now more difficult. We can search for hours or days for a word that has a particular meaning. The attempt to recollect one of your telephone numbers from the past was meant to illustrate this kind of searching. Rigorous memory search can be involved, requiring mental effort, deliberate strategies, rejection of offered possibilities, and sometimes reconstruction of what the answer must be.

Again I turn to the answering of questions to illustrate a point. Some questions can be answered directly. If I ask whether a canary has wings, you might search for that fact directly. Alternatively you might create a mental image of a relevant scene and derive the answer by examining the image. It is also possible that information required may not be directly available but can be derived from other facts that are known. Did the dodo have wings? A dodo was a bird, all birds have wings; therefore a dodo had wings. Those three different ways of answering a question suggest three different types of memory use:

1. Questions that seem to be answered by searching memory for information:
   a. Is a porpoise a mammal or a fish?
   b. How old are you?
   c. What is the capital of New South Wales?

2. Questions that seem to be answered by examining a mental image:
   a. If you fly from Madrid to Berlin, what countries will you pass over?
   b. Does Lincoln's profile on the penny face to the right or left? (Substitute any currency you wish that has a face on it.)
   c. How many windows are there in the place where you live?

3. Questions that seem to be answered by inference:
   a. Does a male whale have a penis?
   b. Are there more piano tuners in New York City or in Tokyo?
   c. Does an elephant eat more food in a day than a lion?

Three separate categories of questions, three different types of memory use. I do not claim that these three uses are independent or exhaustive, or that every question illustrates the particular type of retrieval used by every reader of this book, but I will claim that most readers used several search methods in seeking answers for the nine questions and that most of them were similar to the three types of memory use I described.

Just how questions are answered has been the focus of research both by psychologists and by those who study artificial intelligence. In the process a considerable amount has been learned about memory search and about inference. Not so much is known about mental images. Some people claim mental images are of great importance in their thoughts, others claim never to have experienced such an image—a matter I shall come back to later.

7

Forgetting

What were the names of all my schoolteachers, from kindergarten through high school? I cannot remember, try as I may. The information cannot be found.

Remembering, as I noted earlier, requires the acquisition, retention, and retrieval of information. Forgetting refers to any failure to retrieve and includes the act of forgetting today but remembering tomorrow.

My failure to recover the names of grade-school teachers could not have stemmed from a failure to acquire the information. I must have known those names well at one time. The problem therefore must lie in the retention or in the retrieval of the information. But how can we distinguish between a retention failure (which would be a true loss of information) and an inability to retrieve that information? There is no way, as long as the names cannot be retrieved. There are suspicions, however, that the names are really still in memory but buried under all else that is there. The evidence is weak, mostly circumstantial, but whenever people try hard enough and long enough to remember names and details of the past, a surprising amount can be recovered.

A major problem in retrieval from the past has to do with the structure of memory and the large amount of material contained within it. Consider your memory for last evening's dinner. With minimal effort you can probably remember the food, the setting, where you sat, and what you did. If you ate with others, you can probably recall where they sat and the nature of your interactions. Now try to do the same for the dinner you had on this date exactly 10 years ago.

You forget the meals of the past, sometimes even the ones you wish to remember. In the last 10 years you have eaten approximately 10,000 meals. Even if the most intimate details of all those meals are still in secondary memory, how is it possible to get back any particular experience? The details all blur into a generalized concept of meals. My attempt to find the specific dinner I ate exactly one year ago is diminished by the sheer confusion of all those other similar events. It would take a unique identification tag on that dinner to make it accessible.

Successful retrieval requires more than storage. The desired event must be described in a way that distinguishes it from all others with which it might become confused. Unless the description is sufficiently well specified, the retrieval will fail; the information is not accessible. It might as well not be in memory, since it cannot be found amidst the clutter.

There are other kinds of forgetting. I intend to mail a letter on the way to work. I forget, remembering only when I reach home later in the day and discover the letter sitting on my desk. This could be a failure of retention. It is possible that the intention never got beyond primary memory.

A third kind of forgetting is related to the second but is more complex. I do take the letter, but I fail to mail it. I might "remember" that I intended to mail the letter at periodic intervals during the day, but never when I was in a position to do so. At the end of the day I have failed to mail the letter, but now the matter is not just a simple failure to acquire information in secondary memory. This instance is more complex because it requires an understanding of the human action system. How do we perform any actions? In part I believe we formulate an intention that then guides the act. In this case, the intention was active, but only within primary memory; because the capacity of this system is limited, eventually the intention goes away. Hence the forgetting is due in part to the inopportune timing of the intention.

That example leaves us with a puzzle. Why does someone remember to mail a letter at all? What causes me, at a random time in the day, suddenly to think: "The letter. I must mail the letter." This kind of remembering is reminding, which is perhaps the complement to forgetting. Why is one reminded of things at apparently random moments?

My belief is that random reminding does not occur, that the memory structures are such that even apparently chance thoughts can always be traced to a logical network interrelating the ideas, much as my musing through my own memory structures led me from the shower in Champaign to thoughts of a party to trays for my slide projector. (Here I follow Freud: "Nothing in the mind is arbitrary or undetermined," is how he put it.)

"Out of sight, out of mind," is an old saying, but one with considerable validity. To remember to mail a letter, you must be reminded by something.

Perhaps the thoughts of the day will automatically lead to the mailing at an opportune time, but it would be better to put the letter in some visible place so that the sight would trigger the thought.

How do we remember to turn off the headlights when we leave the car? In the dark, the sight of the lights will remind us. In the daytime, the lack of a visible reminder can lead to the lack of remembering: the lights stay on.

If you are piloting an airplane, how do you remember to lower your landing gear when it is time to land? When you work around the house, do you remember to clean up all the tools, or to reset the circuit breakers or temperature settings that you had to change, or to turn the house water back on? Turning off the water supply to the house and forgetting to reopen it is a simple error caused by a loss of information in primary memory. It becomes a serious error when an airplane pilot does not lower the landing gear, or when the valves that were not reopened are part of the secondary cooling system of a nuclear reactor. All these errors have happened. They all result from commonplace, simple forgetting.

There are other reasons for forgetting. Yes, I forgot to mail the letter. A simple case of forgetting. But what if it just happened to be convenient not to send the letter? What if I were inviting an unwanted person to a party and delay meant the invitation would not arrive in time? What if I fail to remember only those things that I find uncomfortable? How much more pleasant life would be if we could have selective memory for only those events that were pleasant.

Repression is the clinical name for those forms of forgetting. It serves a useful protective function, preventing unpleasant thoughts from intruding on conscious experience. Repression is an interesting phenomenon. How might it work? Suppose you had a traumatic incident—call it T. How could the memory system avoid retrieving T? One way would be for the memory system to have a censoring device as part of the retrieval mechanism, such that if T were ever about to be retrieved, the censor would balk, stopping the operation. But then the censor would have to know about T, and if other things were to be repressed, the censor would need to know all of them. It would need some powerful interpretive machinery as well, to prevent all possible remembrances of T. In addition the censor would have to operate at a subconscious level, or else we would become aware of T through our awareness of what was being censored.

Another possible censoring mechanism involves marking the memory itself, putting some tag on T that indicates that it is not to be retrieved. This view of the procedure has both virtues and difficulties. If you imagine the marker as some sort of activation, perhaps one that can spread to related concepts, you can soon imagine that the attempt to repress T represses a group of related concepts. This result does occur. Other mechanisms are also possible.

Repression is a simple form of clinical forgetting. There are other, more dramatic, cases, such as clinical amnesia, in which a whole section of a person's life is forgotten. Sometimes amnesia leads to fugue states in which a person lives one life for a while, then switches personalities. The switching can continue back and forth between several different states for many years.

These are complicated phenomena, somewhat beyond my understanding. I can imagine numerous explanations for them, but this is not an area in which I am knowledgeable.

8

The Design of a Memory

One way to get insight into the operation of human memory is to attempt to design an artificial memory system. All memory storage systems containing large quantities of information share some common problems. These result from the basic task of memory and are independent of the kind of storage system—human, library, or machine.

Suppose you had to design a library system to house the internal memorandums of the United States government. The library is to be used by a large variety of scholars, each with specific interests. The library must provide access to all memorandums in a systematic, intelligent form, so that a scholar could discover, say, the relationship between the farm failures of the 1920s and the current foreign policy on economic support for underdeveloped countries.

There are going to be voluminous masses of memos, so it is important that there be some order to the filing structure. How might this be accomplished? One thing seems clear: unless duplicate copies are made, each memo can be stored in only one place, yet research scholars need to gain access to it by different paths. Thus whatever the organization of the actual documents, no single one will suffice; external keying, referencing, and indexing schemes are necessary. Moreover, because it is not possible to determine beforehand the questions that individual researchers will raise, it is also quite unlikely that any single indexing scheme will prove sufficiently flexible.

How can researchers gain access to the stored material? To answer that question, consider the kind of answers one wants from a memory. Basically, the types of requests expected can be divided into several categories of specification: feature, content, function.

The first category, specification by feature, allows a researcher to look for documents that meet certain organizational specifications. The request might be for a document written by a specific person or produced by a specific organization. It might be for a document written during a specific time period. The important aspect of feature requests is that they specify characteristics of the document, not its contents. No one has to read the document in order to file it or find it—the contents are irrelevant.

The next category is specification by content. Here the document is stored according to its meaning, including topics discussed and statements made. Now very little need be known about the characteristics of the document, but someone must read and interpret its contents in order to file it.

The third category is specification by function. Note the difference between content and function. The document whose specific function is to cause American steel producers to lower their prices might not mention steel at all. The function of the document can be established only by interpreting its contents in view of national events that were taking place when it was written. (In many ways, function requests are an amalgamation of the information specified by feature requests and by content requests.) The organization of a library in terms of the function of documents may continually change as new information or new interpretations of national events cause the perceived function of the documents to change.

The problems of organizing a library system are analogous to the problems of understanding human memory. We store millions or billions of experiences. At the time of the initial experience, we may not know the ways in which we will need to retrieve it later. The question is to discover just what organizational principles are used.

Human memory may very well be organized so as to find things specified by all three types of requests—feature, content, and function. Specification by feature seems to yield the readiest accessibility. Notice how effortlessly and rapidly the words we perceive while reading are deciphered. The perceptual processes provide a set of visual features for the mechanisms that decipher a word and provide its meaning. By contrast, content specification, as in going from the meaning to the discovery of a word, can be slow and difficult. What is the name of the large ungainly bird that brings luck to sailors? This type of retrieval (as devotees of crossword puzzles can attest) is far harder than going from the features of a word—for example, *albatross*— to its meaning.

When we use memory to do problem solving or thinking, the specification of the information that is desired must be internally generated, perhaps provided by other memory structures. But how can we specify what is needed from memory without knowing something about the information that is being specified? The answer is, we can't. To use memory from internally based information there must be a starting point, something must be known about what is sought. There must be a description of the characteristics of the desired target. Perhaps we seek a particular relationship to something already known, perhaps we seek a special feature, perhaps a special function. Whatever, the search for information must start with a memory specification that serves to describe the information that is being sought, and the description will succeed only insofar as it satisfies several criteria:

1. It must refer to something—memory records that satisfy the description must actually exist.

2. It must be sufficiently precise—a vague description will match too much in memory to be usable.

3. It must allow for verification—if several records satisfy the description, there must be a way of selecting among them.

4. The description must be in a form that the memory-access mechanisms can use—an obvious but necessary requirement.

Suppose that as I write this book I wish to retrieve the title and author of a report about a person with extraordinary memory abilities. How does that desire lead to the steps necessary for the memory search and retrieval?

The statement of my desire is a description of the items sought. In general, such descriptions supply two things: a starting point and a verification procedure. Whether the search will be productive depends critically on the relationship of the description to the way in which the relevant information is stored within me. Let us call the desired records of information in memory the targets.

The process of retrieval from a large memory structure is going to require several subprocesses, each used repeatedly until the desired item is found (or the search is given up). Four different subprocesses can be identified: retrieval specification, matching, evaluation, and failure diagnosis. These are shown in Table 8-1.

The action of the four subprocesses can be illustrated by my attempt to retrieve the title and author of that report about a person with extraordinary memory abilities. Here is where I started:

Retrieval specification: The target record is

Item: book or technical paper

Style: case history

Topic: person with exceptional memory

Place and Additive Memory Systems

There are two fundamentally different ways of storing information in artificial memory systems. The more convenient way puts each memory record in a separate location; this is the *place system*. The other has just one massive place, and all records get added together, one on top of the other; this is the *additive system*.

A typical place system is a filing cabinet (with each memory record in a separate file) or a library (where the separate books are at different shelf locations and the indexes have separate cards for each index or record), a digital computer (where words of the memory or locations on magnetic disc or tape serve as the special places for different items of information). Almost all contemporary artificial storage systems are of the place variety.

Place memories can be implemented in a wide variety of ways, but all have certain basic difficulties of organization and of access. Chief among these is "the address problem": to get at the desired information, its "place" or "address" must be known. The solution is to have many indexes and thesauruses, cross-references and links, all helping to trace down the address of the sought-for information.

In the additive system, different memory records are superimposed on top of one another. The best known of these systems is the hologram, but this is a special case of a general class of additive devices. In the hologram, it is possible to superimpose many different pictures on the same photographic plate.

Recovery from additive memories takes advantage of the mathematical property of independence, or orthogonality. If the pieces of each record are properly chosen, it is likely that the piece from one record has nothing to do with the pieces of the other records: the pieces are orthogonal. And, by proper mathematical operations, the desired image can be retrieved while all the rest of the material that

All this provides a partial description of the desired item. With this description I enter memory and retrieve some records. My initial retrieval went something like this:

Umm, that article—several articles really—about that British mathematician, what's-his-name. Written by a British psychologist. Appeared in the *British Journal of Psychology*, I think. Reprinted several places. Just saw a new version. George Miller was the first person to show it to me, a long time ago. Exceptional ability to do mental is stored in the same place just adds random noise (or jitter) to the record, a random noise that tends to get very small under appropriate conditions.

The additive system is relatively immune to damage because the information is scattered all around. In a place memory, damage to part of the memory loses all the information that has been placed there.

Additive memories are marvelous devices for access via contents. Insert partial contents of the record sought and out comes the entire record. Illuminate a hologram with coherent light that has been modulated with part of the image being sought, and the entire image is revealed. Other forms of retrieval questions create difficulties, however. What is the name of the current prime minister of Canada? How is this information to be got at? What about the use of the information for thought and for problem solving? Additive memory systems have been proposed as models of human memory, but my personal belief is that such proposals are premature. Additive memory systems are too good at content-addressable retrieval, too slow at organizational questions.

Basically, contemporary place memory systems are superior at tracing out relationships among items and additive memories are superior at content access. The distributed nature of additive memories makes them more tolerant to damage than are contemporary place memories, but this feature is a result of the distribution of information, not of the additive aspect of memory.

Work on additive memory systems has just begun. They offer attractive memory structures, but they do not solve the pressing organizational problems of human memory that are my main concern here and that exist independent of the type of memory system used for storage.

arithmetic. But wait a minute, that's not memory. So it doesn't matter—that's not what I'm looking for.

There was an initial retrieval of an item that fitted the description "a case history of a person with an exceptional x." The information retrieved was incomplete, and in my attempt to get to the name of the person (and the places where the reports were published), an evaluation process took place. The result was the realization that the papers were about computational ability, not memory ability, and so the record was not relevant. The evaluation

Table 8-1
Four subprocesses of memory retrieval

Subprocess	Input to subprocess	Output from subprocess
Retrieval specification	Purposes Needs Partial descriptions Perceptual descriptions	*Target description *Verification criteria
Matching	Target description	Memory records
Evaluation	Verification criteria Memory records	*Success or failure: If success, terminate If failure, diagnose
Failure diagnosis	Information from evaluation process	Revised retrieval specification

*May require memory retrieval.

process reports failure, and so the search must start again. Note that I could tell the retrieved item was wrong even without precisely recalling the item itself; an evaluation of the results of the search was sufficient.

The failure diagnosis didn't help me to reformulate the retrieval specification, except to suggest that perhaps the focus of the search should not be on case histories but on memory ability.

Continued attempt at retrieval was more revealing. I suddenly thought of the studies by the late Soviet psychologist Luria and of the books he had written. Almost immediately the title—*Mind of a Mnemonist*—came to mind. I had my item. But my thoughts continued:

> Luria, *Mind of a Mnemonist*. The story of S; strange person, could remember unbelievable detail. Major problem in life was that he could not forget. S stands for, umm, a long Russian name. Umm, it's not given in the book itself, Luria only identified him as S. But I know who it really was; it's common knowledge. It's . . . I know I wrote it down somewhere, perhaps in my copy of Luria's book.

That was successful retrieval. It passed the memory evaluation, because I could recall sufficient information to see that it was consistent with the retrieval specification. I had my target item, and, as shown in the table, I could now terminate the search.

But I didn't stop. I remembered that the psychologist Earl Hunt once studied a mnemonist, a person he too called by a single initial. Where was that study published? I could not recall. In a chapter of a book? In a journal article? Maybe in both. Was it in *Cognitive Psychology*? I would have to look.

The memory retrieval process, once started, is not easy to stop. Conscious intent starts it off, but subconscious mechanisms seem to persist on their own. As I type this description the name Aiken comes to mind. Why?

Now more comes: Aiken and a book of readings edited by the British psychologists Wason and Johnson-Laird. Aiken is the mathematician I thought of in my first retrieval (I think). Why am I still thinking of that? I interrupt my typing (literally, right here) and get my copy of Wason and Johnson-Laird. Aha, there is an article by Hunter about A. C. Aitken, "the distinguished mathematician . . . of Edinburgh University." Aitken, with a *t*. I got the name wrong, but I was close. Skimming the article, I see that at the end it speaks of Luria's subject, *S:* S. V. Shereshevski. Hunter points out that he compared the memories of Aitken and *S* in a paper published in 1977. Did I see the paper? Is that one reason I was able to remember the Luria book? I do not know.

The memory processes of search are not available to conscious inspection. Because they continued here long after I had thought was necessary, the relation between the two studies may have existed in my memory, unknown to me. And now, having read of the connection between Aitken and Shereshevski, I cannot distinguish between my fresh, current knowledge and any prior existing memory of that same knowledge.

Note that search in memory works only if the description is both appropriate and discriminating. If I ask a librarian for a target record whose description is simply "the item I want is a book," I will get no assistance. The description is appropriate but not discriminating. For a human information storage system, describing the wanted item as a book is actually of some help in restricting the area of search, but for a library storage system, such a description is of little use beyond eliminating periodicals, tapes, newspapers and maps.

Consider the fuller statement "the item I want is a book about a Soviet mnemonist." The description is still inappropriate and using it to enter the index system and catalogues of most libraries will yield no information whatsoever. For my colleagues, however, the description is sufficient. If they know the book at all, the description is appropriate and discriminating enough to get to the book. Only one such book is known to most cognitive psychologists.

The properties of description are relative to the organization and content of the memory system to which they are applied. Moreover, a description that suffices at one time will not necessarily suffice later on. Thus the description of my house as "the white house with the bright red door" will be sufficiently discriminating only as long as my neighbors do not repaint their houses similarly. A description for an event such as "the time I beat Marigold at table tennis" will suffice to retrieve that unique event from my memory, because I am unlikely ever to win again. Descriptions have one more important property: they must be recoverable. Suppose I am beginning to learn to play the piano, and I am learning the notes of the treble clef. In order, the notes positioned on the five horizontal lines of the staff are E, G, B, D, F. I learn a simple mnemonic for the notes, the first letter of each word in the phrase "Every good boy does fine." The mnemonic is a description—now the only problem is to retrieve the phrase. That is, the problem is with the recoverability of the description.

The preceding examples tell only part of the story of our use of memory, the part dealing with the search for particular information. More often, however, the information we seek is not within the memory structures but must be deduced, constructed as a logical conclusion of information that we do have. In that case, we must use the information within memory as a guide toward the construction of the information that we seek. Understanding something of the deduction process requires insight into how knowledge may be represented in the memory system. And so now I want to look at two related concepts that have been proposed by students of philosophy, psychology, and artificial intelligence: semantic networks and memory schemas. As usual, I start with the attempt to answer a question.

9

Semantic Networks

Suppose that space explorers discover a planet with inhabitants that look like us. Is it likely that these alien people eat food?

The question has no correct answer, but a good guess requires reasoning about the nature of food and people. I shall eventually arrive at an answer—several answers, in fact—but I am going to drag out the discussion, because the question is really just an excuse to consider what kind of memory structures might make possible the reasoning required for an answer.

To start with, let me simplify the question by asking some related ones. All the questions are about J, a person whom you have never met. All you know about J must be inferred.

Question 1: Does J have two legs?

Answer 1: Probably. J is a person and people normally have two legs. So unless J is abnormal (or has had an accident), J has two legs.

Question 2: Does J eat food?

Answer 2: Of course. J is a person, and a person is an animal, and all animals eat; the substance animals eat is called food.

Question 2A: Well, what if J were in a coma or on a hunger strike? And are you sure that all animals eat? What about a newly hatched chick?

Answer 2A: You're getting awfully technical. We're really just talking about people. All people eat, everyone knows that. That's why a coma or a hunger strike is an exception—it violates a biological necessity. Maybe I should have said that all people must eat or somehow get fed, or within a few weeks they will die.

Question 3:   Does *J* have mass?

Answer 3:   What peculiar questions you ask! *J* is a person and all people have bodies. I could prove it to you, I guess. *J*'s body is a physical object, and all physical objects have mass. Okay?

   Those simple questions get to the heart of the matter. Consider the simple, obvious responses to the three basic questions: yes, yes, and yes. People have two legs, they eat food, and their bodies have mass. These are the obvious answers, in a sense the "correct" answers. The difficulty is that I can think of special cases where the answers don't apply, as the qualifications in Answer 1 and the exchange of Question 2A indicate. Somehow a theory of memory structure must include both aspects of these answers: that there is an immediate, obvious answer and that we are capable of prolonged examination and qualification of almost any answer. But for now let's see what kind of memory structures can be used for obvious answers.

   The obvious way to answer Questions 1, 2, and 3 is to identify *J* as an instance of a class—person, animal, physical object—then determine the properties of the class, and conclude that all its members must share the properties. To do this we need a means of representing class membership, a means of representing the properties of classes, and a means of using those representations to answer questions. One useful tool is a semantic network, a structure in which relevant pieces of information are linked together in appropriate ways.

   Semantic networks provide a way of representing the relationships among the concepts and events in a memory system. Semantic networks produce a fair description of our reasoning process. But there is a vast difference between proposing a theoretical account of human thought and memory processes and actually determining that the account provides a satisfactory explanation. Although semantic networks are a useful tool, they have been shown to have inadequacies in their description of human behavior, and so they have been modified in ways that I shall discuss later. The theoretical and experimental explorations of the possible range of representational formats are in their infancy. So read the following with caution—semantic networks are a powerful tool that captures much of the human reasoning processes, but they are hypothesis, not fact.

   Figure 9-1 shows a semantic network that allows us to get to the obvious answer to the question about the number of legs *J* has. It represents the information that *J* is a person and that people have two legs.

The important parts of the network are the *nodes* and *relations*. In *J isa person*, *J* and *person* are nodes, and *isa* is a relation meaning *is an instance of*. *J* is an instance of the concept of person. The *property* of having two legs is represented in similar fashion; the relation *has-as-part* holds between *person* and ⟨*two legs*⟩. (The angle brackets signify that the node for *two legs* is not a concept in the same manner as *person*; actually the representation for *two legs* should be a bit more complex than is shown here.)

Now Question 1—Does *J* have two legs?—can be answered by using the network. *J isa person*, a *person has-as-part two legs*, therefore *J has-as-part two legs*.

Question 2—Does *J* eat food?—is answered by a similar process, but the information required must be expanded into the form shown in Figure 9-2.

In the expanded network I introduce a few new types of relations. First, there is the *subset* relation, similar in function to *isa*, but meaning that the concept of person is a subset of the concept of animal. The node that is represented by the oval is more complex. An oval node is the basic format of a proposition. In the example given, the oval node means that the concept pointed to by the relation labeled *a* eats the concept pointed to by the relation

Figure 9-1.

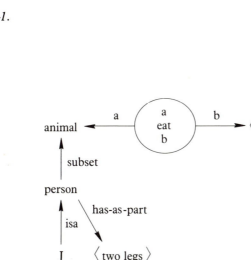

Figure 9-2.

labeled *b*. The node represented by ⟨*100⟩ indicates the concept of the stuff that is eaten, which, in turn, is an instance of food. The angle brackets are required because a particular animal doesn't eat all foods, just certain foods. And so ⟨*100⟩ *isa food*; in other words, ⟨*100⟩ stands for instances of the class of things called food. (The name *100 means nothing; it is a label so that I can refer to the concept.)

An important property of semantic networks is *inheritance*. Properties of a concept are inherited by its descendants, that is, its instances and subsets. If *A* is an instance or a subset of *B*, and if *B* has relationship *r* to *C*, then *A* has relationship *r* to *C* (Figure 9-3).

There is one more question about *J*, Question 3—Does *J* have mass? Two paths to the answer are shown. *J* is a person and people have bodies; bodies are objects that have mass. Alternatively *J* is a person, which is, in turn, both a mammal and an animal, a living thing and an object. And all physical objects have mass (Figure 9-4).

Semantic networks have proved to be powerful devices for representing knowledge and for guiding inference. One of the powers of semantic networks is the richness of the relationships that they can depict. Note that these networks are not restricted to such hierarchies as "a person is an animal and animals are living things." The hierarchy can be broken, as in the figure where I have shown that a person is both a mammal and an animal.

It is possible to go far beyond these simple networks. I can add thousands (or millions) of statements together, each in the form of the simple node-relation-node triple. I can show you how to draw pictures of the relationships that form elaborate knowledge networks. Soon a logic will begin to operate on the networks, allowing you to deduce that bread has mass, that a canary

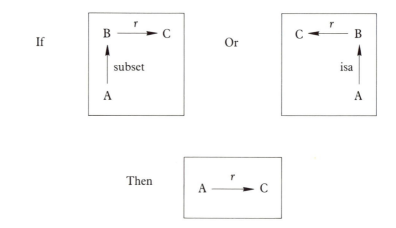

Figure 9-3.

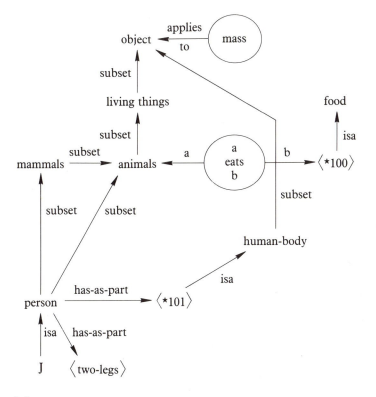

Figure 9-4.

must also have mass, that a song does not. The knowledge contained in the networks will become more and more elaborate. I can incorporate contradictions and exceptions: All birds can fly, except for the penguin, the ostrich, and a few others. Soon the networks will become powerful enough to state the functions of things and to reveal the complex structures of complex things. The networks will become larger and larger. If they are allowed to grow unchecked, they will engulf the book (which is reasonable, for the knowledge in my head that allowed me to write this book must surely be more than is in the book). The result will be an immense compilation of knowledge that is capable of supporting intelligent deduction and of expressing the profound and the trivial. Soon it will be hard to follow the networks, for they will be so big that they cannot be seen in their entirety. The networks will indeed take on a life of their own.

As a theoretician and scientist interested in the properties of human memory, I am now placed in an interesting dilemma. On the one hand, the problems of representing knowledge are important and the properties of semantic networks and related systems are intriguing, worthy of study and of continued elaboration. On the other hand, all this speculation has got us rather far from what can easily be tested concerning the properties of human memory. How does one proceed? Is it possible to test the ideas I've presented? Are they sheer abstractions or do they have some basis in the actual operations of human memory? How can we tell?

At this point, scientific philosophies diverge. Some psychologists believe strongly that things have already gone too far and that each theoretical step should be checked meticulously by experimentation before any new step is taken. I disagree. I believe the pursuit of the mechanisms of knowledge representation is important for two reasons. First, study of these is important in its own right, as pure cognitive science, even if they should ultimately prove to be unrealistic as an account of human memory. Cognitive science must investigate the range of possible theories, regardless of their empirical status. If we understand the range of possible representational structures, we will be better able to assess those of the human (or of animals or of artificial devices).

Second, I believe these ideas should be tested only after the range of their potential implications and strengths has been explored in depth. It is premature to experiment on initial ideas. One of the major tests of a theory is whether it has sufficient power to explain the phenomena that are of interest. This is called the test of sufficiency. To know whether a theory is sufficient, it is necessary to pursue it in some detail. It is likely that many changes will have to be made to achieve sufficiency.

Once sufficiency has been established, the experimental tests can begin, tests that establish the necessity of the theory. Eventually all theories of human thought processes must pass the tests of both sufficiency and necessity. The tests will be made easier, however, if we first understand the range of possible theories. Then, and only then, is it possible to make comparisons among competing theories.

Semantic networks are powerful tools and they were the starting point for much of the current research. But they have already been modified substantially. So, without discussing what can (or cannot) be experimentally verified, I shall proceed in the examination of the properties of a representational system. But first we must modify semantic networks to allow for larger units of knowledge. The result is the method called the schema.

Recall the question, Do the people who inhabit the newly discovered planet eat food? How can we reach an answer with semantic networks? And how can we get beyond the obvious answers to ones with more depth and validity? We can't, at least not without some strategies for determining how old knowledge can be applied to new situations. The processes that make use of knowledge are as important as the knowledge itself. Indeed, they are themselves knowledge—knowledge of doing instead of knowledge about.

10

Schemas:
Packets of Knowledge

What do we know about food that can guide us toward an answer to the question asked in the last chapter about the people on the other planet? To eat, according to my copy of *Webster's New Collegiate Dictionary*, is "to take in through the mouth as food." The mouth, according to this same dictionary, is "the opening through which food passes into the body of an animal." Food is "material . . . used in the body of an organism to sustain growth, repair, and vital processes and to furnish energy." The definitions tend to be circular, but the intent is clear. Here is my version, formed from my own knowledge:

> Eating is the act of ingesting material that enables the biological structures of the body to grow, repair damage, and get sufficient energy to sustain daily activities. The opening of the body through which the material enters is called a mouth, and the material itself is called food.

A packet of information, such as my definition, forms an organized body of knowledge: a schema.

Schemas represent a more advanced level of knowledge than the simple structures of semantic networks, and they add considerable power to representational theory. Schemas supplement semantic networks in several ways.

Essentially schemas are integrated bodies of knowledge that are relevant to a limited domain. Thus we might have schemas about books or about the structure of typewriter keyboards, or schemas that describe the hitting of a baseball. Schemas form individual packets of knowledge that consist of highly interrelated knowledge structures (perhaps with the contents being represented, in part, by a small semantic network).

The theory of schemas is not yet fully developed. In the latter part of this book I examine some of the proposed properties of schemas while discussing possible changes in students' knowledge structures as they learn a complicated topic. For now it is enough to state some basic properties. Schemas may contain both knowledge and rules for using knowledge. Schemas can be composed of references to other schemas, so that the schema for writing instruments refers to the schema for typewriters, which in turn refers to schemas for typewriter components, such as the schema for the keyboard. Schemas can be specific (the schema for my personal typewriter) or general (the schema for a typical typewriter, related to, but different from the specific schema for my typewriter).

How might schemas help answer the question about whether the alien people eat? Food supplies materials and energy to an organism, allowing it to repair itself, to grow, and to carry on other processes. Do alien people grow in size as they mature? Can they repair injuries by new growth? Do they need energy to exist? We can't answer the first two questions (although we can make plausible guesses), but we can answer the last one. Anything or anyone who performs an active function—such as moving or thinking or just maintaining body temperature at some value different from that of the environment—requires energy. If the aliens do any of these things, they must use energy. But do they have to eat?

The answer is yes and no. If the aliens need to replenish the energy they expend, then they must take in some form of energy. If the energy comes from food, then there must be an orifice—a mouth. Of course, that is not the only possible answer. What schemas do we have for the intake of energy without a mouth? I can think of at least two. The energy could be electromagnetic or it could come from a liquid or gas that was absorbed by the skin or outside layers of the body without any identifiable mouth.

The first answer sounds best. Tentatively I conclude that, yes, aliens eat and have mouths, a way of getting the food into their mouths, and a way of disposing of waste products (I doubt that aliens are 100 percent efficient in extracting energy from food).

Of course there might be still other ways of getting energy. The aliens might have evolved to be something like our automobiles, so that every 30 days they pull up before the stalks of the great fluid-plant and insert the stalk of the plant into an opening in the top of their bodies. The plant drips an organic fluid into the opening. Can that be called eating? Is the fluid food?

Alternatively, let the aliens undergo metamorphosis from vegetable to animal. In the first two years of life they grow as vegetables. When they reach full size, they break loose from their stalks and transform into animals—into people. From then on, they live on the energy accumulated within their bodies during the plant phase. As they grow older they grow smaller, until they wither away and die. In their mature form, they do not eat food (or eliminate waste).

The point of that whole exercise, of course, is that reaching conclusions requires more than simple use of memory skills. Existing knowledge must be examined, reformulated, reapplied. Storing a desired piece of information and getting back what was put there earlier are the most obvious uses of a memory, but these are perhaps the least important aspects of it.

11

Schemas, Scripts, and Prototypes

Semantic networks and schemas are two closely related theoretical proposals for the representation of information in memory. Each has virtues, and so a complete theoretical account is likely to contain both. But networks and schemas alone will not pass the test of sufficiency. More is required. In this chapter and the next, I want to examine certain deficiencies of these methods of representing information and also the proposed expansions of them.

Semantic networks are useful for representing the formal relationships among things—for showing that Sam, my son's Labrador retriever, is a type of dog and that dogs have certain properties and characteristics by virtue of being animals or living things, or physical objects. Networks are most effective wherever classifications can be made in a reasonably straightforward, consistent manner.

Schemas are organized packets of knowledge gathered together to represent single units of self-contained knowledge. My schema for Sam might contain the information that describes his physical features, his activities, and his personality traits. The Sam schema refers to other schemas that describe different aspects of him. Thus one schema is for a prototypical activity: retrieving wooden sticks thrown into the ocean (swimming through the waves to find them and surfing back).

Consider the stick-retrieval schema. The information within it is of several kinds. I said "wooden stick"; will that stick float? You probably assumed it would, making the inference from your knowledge of the properties of wood.

That is the sort of property that can be deduced from semantic networks. So too with the properties of dogs. I assume you imagined a dog with four legs, a tail and all the other properties of dogs in general.

The retrieval story has other aspects to it. There is a typical sequence of events. I find a stick and show it to Sam. He sits beside me as I throw it as far as possible into the ocean. At a signal, Sam charges after the stick. If he fails to find it, he swims in circles, first moving steadily towards me, then steadily away. Eventually he either finds the stick or (rarely) returns without it. He runs up to me, stops a few feet away, drops the stick, shakes himself off, picks up the stick and brings it to my waiting hand (a most amazing dog, Sam).

My memory for this activity is a combination of specific features and general overviews of the retrieving behavior. In any particular throw Sam may not wait for the signal, and it may take several tries before Sam drops the stick into my hand. Yet when I first run through Sam's beach activities mentally, the simpler, stereotyped version is the one I recall. Sam's behavior is regular, routine. I feel as if we are playacting—each of us doing his part. The two of us engage in a number of pleasant rituals.

Such ritualization of behavior has impressed various theoreticians. It is as if we have a collection of scripts, and for many situations we simply pull out the appropriate one and follow it; "scripts," "games," or "frames" are the names given to these ritualized patterns. One analytic technique—transactional analysis—is based on this notion; *Games People Play* is the title of a popular book on the subject. Some memory theorists have also explored the idea that much human behavior—and memory of that behavior—is governed by scripts. The word "script" is used here in a technical sense that is only partially consistent with the normal dictionary definition of the term, for it is not like a script for a play, in which every word or action is carefully spelled out. Rather, it refers to the general specifications of the ordering of the activities and to the interactions among the participants of the event. The basic idea is that some sequences follow relatively fixed patterns, fixed as if they were written in a script that guides the behavior. Such scripts allow the observer of an event to predict what will happen next; in the case of a new instance of a common event, the script provides guidance on how to proceed. Thus Sam's behavior with a stick or events at a restaurant or at a physician's office tend to follow routinized patterns. The proposal is that human memory structures contain scriptlike knowledge units that allow the interpretation and prediction of ongoing events and the storage and the recovery of the remembrance of a prior event.

Consider how the broad outlines of a restaurant script might go. You enter the restaurant and find an empty table, sometimes by yourself, sometimes by waiting for someone to direct you. You sit, then wait. Eventually a waiter arrives to give you a menu (and in the United States, a glass of water). The waiter leaves, then returns a while later to take your order. In due course, the waiter brings the food, which you eat. Then the waiter brings your bill, and you pay either the waiter or a cashier. You leave a tip, even if you were not satisfied with the meal.

Everyone knows of exceptions to the restaurant script. In some restaurants you pay first, and then get the food. In others you sign a slip and don't pay until the end of the month. Sometimes the behavior of the waiter is predictably different. Cafeterias are different. Restaurants in other countries are different. One might require several different scripts to capture the variations—perhaps 10 or 12 (but, say the true believers in scripts, not 100 or 1000). I find it reasonable that a few restaurant scripts can capture a large set of common experiences. Moreover, when I enter a restaurant that is new to me, I examine it, look at the other diners, at the waiters, at the organization of the interior. I attempt to decide how to behave (in cafeterias I seat myself: in other restaurants I wait to be seated, and so on). Once I classify the restaurant type, I know the script, I know what to do. If I turn out to be wrong, that discrepancy is noteworthy enough to draw the attention of other diners.

It is surprising how much of human behavior seems to follow simple scripts: going to the motion pictures, going to the library, going to a dentist or a physician, a classroom lecture, a business lunch.

The concept of scripts is subject to some debate. On the one hand, scripts are useful as a rough guide to much human activity. On the other hand, they seem too rigid and simplistic to capture real situations. They have, however, turned out to be useful tools for researchers in the artificial intelligence community who are working with computer programs that interact with users in intelligent ways. Researchers at Yale University have categorized many types of global events into various scripts. They have simple scripts for the events that occur during major earthquakes, government crises, economic boycotts, and civil strife. This knowledge of events has been put into a computer program that has sufficient knowledge of English to read the wire-service news releases, categorize the events into one of the script classifications, and then send out general messages to anyone in the laboratory who is interested: "Earthquake in Guatemala," "OPEC raises oil prices," "terrorists seize airport," "Iran recalls its ambassador." For each news story there is a brief synopsis based on the script for the event. The program simply fills in the particulars, thereby providing simple summaries of the world's events from the actual texts produced by the wire services, doing it on-line, responding even as the news bulletins arrive over the telephone connection. Do human beings do things in this way? I doubt it, but scripts strike me as a useful first approximation, one small step of the many we must take.

Whatever the status of scripts as a theoretical construct in the understanding of human memory, the notion does attempt to capture one of the more important aspects of human knowledge: that our impressions of events follow routinized, stereotypical patterns. Scripts provide one method of representing such patterning. Similar arguments apply to our knowledge of concepts. Indeed, one of the most potent criticisms of research on semantic networks is that they fail to capture the notion of sterotypicality.

Semantic networks were designed to indicate the relationships that hold among concepts. They are quite successful at doing that, but from the point of view of the psychologist who is concerned with the modeling of human memory, they are too successful, too powerful. Thus, according to a simple interpretation of semantic networks, once one learns that a sponge is an animal, that knowledge can be encoded in exactly the same way as the knowledge that a wolf is an animal. And that is the problem.

Is a sponge an animal? Well, sure it is. We all learn that information somewhere. But unless we are experienced in zoological matters, the fact that a sponge is an animal is simply not as salient or as comfortable a piece of knowledge as the fact that a wolf is an animal.

Consider the following animals:

wolf

person

penguin

sponge

The list of animals is ordered in terms of their "goodness of fit" to the concept of animal. The ordering is suggestive of a representation; it is somewhat as if there were a prototypical, or "ideal," animal, with the judgment of the goodness of fit of an example being determined by how far away it is from the ideal. Experimental studies support that conception. For middle-class college students in northern California, the ideal animal turns out to be something like a wolf or a dog. Interestingly, the ideal mammal is essentially the same; for the students, the concepts of "animal" and "mammal" are very closely related. Moreover, they distinguish people and birds from animals.

Although I assume the students tested were fully aware of the proper biological classification of animals, their mental representations divided the kingdom into people, animals, birds, fish, and insects. An animal is something like a wolf. A bird is something like an amalgam of pigeon, sparrow, and robin. A whale is much closer to the prototypical fish than to the prototypical mammal. Certainly that is how my mental structures are organized, even though I know full well that biological classification is quite different. Things like sponges give me trouble. In general, I see sponges as things I buy to clean my house with (and sometimes the "sponges" are made of plastic). I have seen real, live sponges growing on coral in tropical waters, but there they fit neither my conception of an animal nor my conception of a sponge (certainly not a kitchen sponge). My knowledge structures for animals are probably quite neat and orderly when the animals are close to the prototype. My knowledge structures are probably quite messy for nontypical cases, such as spiders and sponges, penguins and bats. A few psychologists have probed deeply into people's understanding of basic concepts and found that they rest on ill-supported, badly confused knowledge structures that are sometimes mutually contradictory. I hate to admit it publicly, but my understanding of some basic concepts is probably also self-contradictory. Probably everyone's knowledge structures are.

The notions of prototypes and of goodness of fit need to be incorporated into the theoretical structure for the representation of knowledge within human memory. Semantic networks don't do a good job of capturing these ideas. What is needed is some mechanism by which the knowledge of one's typical beliefs of the structure of concepts can be encoded, so that each particular instance can then be judged by how closely it conforms to that typical or prototypical belief. Encoding is essentially what one can accomplish with schemas, those organized packets of knowledge discussed earlier. A schema provides the theoretical mechanism for introducing prototypical knowledge for concepts, much as a script introduced the theoretical mechanism for prototypical knowledge for event sequences.

How are schemas and scripts used in the interpretation of everyday events and perceptions and also in the memory for them? The observations about the role of prototypical knowledge provide an important clue. Schemas should be organized around some ideal, or prototype, with considerable information about the concepts they represent, including typical values for various aspects of their components.

Adding the concept of typical values to the schema gives it considerable power, with some unexpected dividends in accounting for human behavior. For example, the schema for "animal" might state that it has exactly one head: for "mammal," that it has four limbs; and for "person," that it has two arms and two legs. The schema for "bird" might state that it flies, and the one for "U.S. mail deposit box," that the box is blue. These typical values serve several functions. First, people do know this information, and they will provide it if asked. Second, and more important, if there is no direct evidence to the contrary, then the typical values seem to apply. Thus if I talk about a dog, you will assume it has a head, four legs, and a tail. In fact, if the dog has only three legs, you will expect me to mention it. In conversation we rely heavily on shared knowledge, so that it is unnecessary to say everything about the topic under discussion.

These typical values are called default values. The name comes from the fact that if there is no specific information to the contrary, the typical values are assumed to apply by default. By default I assume you are between 1½ and 2 meters in height, eat three meals a day (and at their default times), have two legs, and so on. I could be wrong, and if so, I will change those values in the memory schema I construct for you. On the whole, the assumption of default values considerably simplifies processing.

The goodness of fit of any particular experience is given by how well it matches an existing schema. We seem to judge things by goodness of fit to prototypes, and ill-structured prototypes can lead to erroneous interpretations and assumptions.

What happens when we apply schemas to our knowledge of people? Do we have schemas for "fat" people (indicating that they are jovial) and for "intense" people and "stingy" ones? Are schemas the mechanisms of stereotyping? If so, note that stereotyping is, in general, a valuable operation, for it allows rich inferences on the basis of partial knowledge. But stereotypes of people can be an insidious evil, for they can cause the assignment of erroneous default values to someone who is judged to be close to a prototype. What is worse, the prototypes can be used subconsciously, without malicious intent. It doesn't matter much when I erroneously assign characteristics of fishes to whales or of birds to bats. But it can matter a lot to society when I consciously or subconsciously form similar judgments about cultural or ethnic groups of people.

12

Mental Images

The remembering of a past event often carries the feeling that the remembrance is rich, detailed, complete: a version of the original. The notion that memory structures capture an image of the original event is a compelling one that has led to years of active debate and disagreement among those who study memory structures. The argument continues today, the basic issue revolving around the meaning of the term "image."

How many printed lowercase letters of the alphabet have descenders, a part that descends below the line? How many have ascenders, a part that sticks up above the letter? The answers are that five letters have descenders (g, j, p, q, y) and seven letters have ascenders (b, d, f, h, k, l, t). To answer these questions most people must either look at a printed page or generate a mental image of each successive letter of the alphabet, examining the image to see if the letter protrudes below or above the line.

What is a mental image? When I "look" at my mentally generated image of the letter q do I really see a q? Do I use the visual sensory apparatus? Mental images are elusive. Not only is it difficult to get good evidence about their nature, but there are strong differences among individuals. Some people claim to be able to visualize things mentally in vivid color, with sharp, clear impressions of the imagined scene. (Others claim similar skills with other modalities, for example, smell or touch or hearing.) Some people deny that they visualize things mentally, perhaps denying an awareness of any form of mental images, or perhaps admitting to fragmentary feelings of images, more visual than anything else, but nothing like an actual visual perception. (Similar denials exist for all the other sensory modalities.)

Despite the large variability in subjective impressions, some sort of image does seem to be used in determining the answers to questions, especially questions that require the use of time or space. To answer the descenders–ascenders questions, most people admit to a successive scanning of the alphabet. The difference is primarily whether the individual letters are seen in a mental image, or whether they simply give rise to an indescribable "impression" of descending or ascending letters. All the evidence is not yet in, but spatial information certainly seems to be used, in part as a mental image.

All is not well with images, however. Even the most seemingly complete and detailed images can be surprisingly incomplete and erroneous.

Consider the following questions:

1. If you fly from London to Moscow, over what countries do you pass? (Alternatively, if you fly from Denver to Chicago, over what states do you pass?)

For many people, such a question seems to invoke an image. They maintain that the only way to answer it is to construct a mental representation of a map and plot the airline path.

Do people really have mental maps? Let's try a few other questions:

2. As you travel from San Diego, California, to Reno, Nevada, in what direction do you travel?

3. As you travel from the Atlantic Ocean side of the Panama Canal to the Pacific Ocean side, in what direction do you travel?

4. What city or state in the United States is directly west of Madrid, Spain?

The information some of us see in mental images is deceptive. The image is rich, but it may not be as complete and accurate as we think. There are surprising errors. What part of the United States lines up with Madrid, Spain? Most people look for a city in the southern United States—in Florida or Georgia. The answer is New Jersey (Madrid is between New York and Philadelphia). Paris, France, lines up almost exactly with the northern border of the United States. London, England, is just south of Alaska and therefore is north of all the other 49 states. Observations of this kind led Al Stevens, working in my laboratory, to examine how people make directional observations. He asked undergraduates at our campus (in San Diego, California) to make judgments of the relative locations of cities. Some of the questions and responses are shown in Figure 12-1.

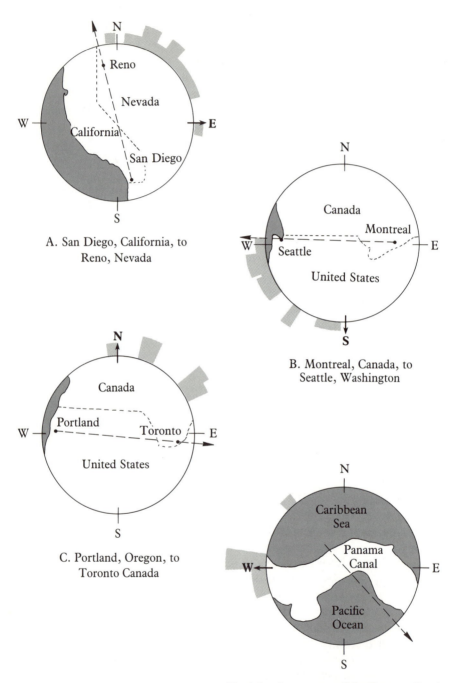

A. San Diego, California, to
   Reno, Nevada

B. Montreal, Canada, to
   Seattle, Washington

C. Portland, Oregon, to
   Toronto Canada

D. Atlantic entrance of the Panama Canal
   to the Pacific entrance

In spite of the fact that many people claim to answer geographical questions through the use of images of the globe or of maps, the answers are most unmaplike. People feel betrayed when they learn the correct answers. Some refuse at first to believe a correct answer, because it contradicts a powerful internal image of the world.

In what direction is Reno from San Diego? Reno is in the middle of Nevada, and San Diego is at the southwest corner of California. California is west of Nevada—hence Reno is northeast of San Diego. Right? Wrong. The reasoning is impeccable, but the fact is that Reno is west of San Diego, not east.

In what direction does one travel through the Panama Canal to get from the Atlantic side to the Pacific side? We all know the Pacific is west of the Atlantic, so it seems that the logical answer is west. The correct answer is that one travels slightly east—south-southeast, to be exact.

Despite those anomalies, there is still a strong impression of the perception of a rich, dense, informative image. If I ask you to form an image of a very tall building and first pose a question about its street level and then about its roof, the amount of time you take to answer the roof question depends partly on how tall your imagined building is. It is as if you had to scan the building, from street to roof, as you would with an actual building. If I ask you to visualize an elephant with a fly on its tail, you will complain of the same difficulty that a photographer would encounter in attempting to photograph the scene. Either the fly is large enough to be visible, in which case only the rear part of the elephant can be seen, or the whole elephant is visible, in which case the fly cannot be seen. The imagined image has many of the same properties as a visual image. Would the schemas that I spoke of earlier present this same problem?

Returning to a basic question, "How is information stored?" I can now give the answer: we don't know. The two major lines of investigation that I have discussed differ in spirit, but they converge in some common themes.

Figure 12-1.
Stevens and Coupe asked people to indicate directions between two well known geographical locations. Four examples are shown in the figure. Consider the question shown in A: In what direction should one travel to go from San Diego to Reno? The map inside the circle and the dashed arrow show the correct answer; the responses are shown by the histogram outside the circle. Responses seem to be strongly affected by superordinate relations: for example, Reno is in the state of Nevada and San Diego in the state of California. Nevada is east of California, hence should not Reno be east of San Diego? The superordinate direction, east, is shown by the solid arrow in the figure. The judgments look like a compromise between the correct direction and the superordinate direction. This compromise holds for all of the questions except for the one dealing with the Panama Canal, where the superordinate answer dominates. [After Stevens and Coupe (1977).]

The first line is the study of propositional representation: the studies of semantic networks and of schemas. This approach is the most complete, sophisticated, and, in my opinion, successful. The relative success is an accident, however. Propositional representations have been studied more thoroughly than the other line. Moreover, they are ideally suited for manipulation as computer data structures, and several programming languages and systems make use of the propositional style of representation. For the analysis of linguistic materials—words, sentences, stories, conversations—propositional representation is well suited.

The second line of investigation concerns the use of mental images. There has been essentially no work on the format of image representation, and so our knowledge of the mechanisms for representing and using images is limited. Most work in psychology has centered around demonstrations of the properties of images, and although the work is invaluable for the eventual development of a full understanding of the representational issues, it is only the first stage.

Images and propositional information must coexist. It must be possible to refer to images through words, through inferences. It must be possible to construct new images from parts of old images, to make inferences, to have images organized in such a way that appropriate ones can be found when they are needed. Propositional representations offer the promise of an explanation of understanding and are ideally suited for inference making. Image information is ideally suited for answering questions about space or time. I suspect that mental images and propositional representation are not as different as some believe, that the two might actually be stored in a common format, and that the appropriate specialized representation is generated for whatever processing needs exist at any given moment. I believe that the errors found in images are the result of the generation of an image for the current purpose and that the underlying storage of the information contains gaps in knowledge that lead to the false inferences.

But I cannot complete this part of the story. Some people believe rather firmly in the existence of spatial images that contain rich, dense information in a two- or three-dimensional array, available for inspection by an internal perceiving device that feeds the information from the array into the mind's eye. Others argue just as vehemently against such a notion, stating that some system of propositional information is all that is involved.

My view is mixed. Although I am a strong advocate of propositional representation, I feel that the information available to me is richer and denser than the information that can be represented in networks or schemas. I argue for local images, small regions of three-dimensional fidelity, tied into some sort of semantic representation. Local information is examined, and when it is found to be insufficient, recourse is made to semantic structures of the kind that tell us that Europe is opposite the United States (so that when I line up things in my mental viewing space, Paris comes out opposite New York—sometimes opposite Washington; Spain lines up with Atlanta, Ga.; Africa is south of the United States; and England is someplace around New England), in spite of the fact that my globe tells me otherwise.

But in truth, neither I nor anyone else knows the answer to the puzzle of mental images. Personally, I think we will not know until there is another breakthrough in our understanding of representation. Some new approach is needed, some new formalization of the problem, the issues, the resolution.

13

Learning
and Skilled Performance

Learning, memory, and performance are interrelated topics. The study of memory tends to emphasize how information is retained and then retrieved for use. The study of learning tends to emphasize the acquisition of information, and the study of performance emphasizes how the information is used.

Learning allows an organism to take in new ideas and to profit from experience. Learning is not a unitary activity. It comes in many shapes and forms. You are learning when you read that the New Orleans police are on strike and so there will be no Mardi Gras. You learn when you try out longer skis and adjust to them. You learn when you read this book.

What does it mean to claim to have learned something? There are several possible answers, depending on how you view the question. Most of the time, learning is closely related to understanding. You have learned to play chess when you understand the moves, the purpose and the basic strategy of the game. When you learn to drive or to sail, you learn something of the mechanics of the situation, something of the rules of the road, and most important, something of the relationship between your actions and the response of the car or boat. From the outsider's point of view, learning is closely related to performance. You may think you understand chess, but if you cannot play a challenging game, I would say you have not really learned it. You may understand how to drive a car, but if you have trouble parking and grind the gears when you shift, I would say you are still in the process of learning to drive.

Skilled performance requires considerable knowledge. But skilled people can sometimes do amazingly well without understanding, and as most of us have found to our sorrow, good knowledge or good understanding does not necessarily lead to good performance. Skilled performance is learned, but the form of learning that transforms one's knowledge into the skilled application of that knowledge is not yet fully understood. Later in this book I cover various aspects of learning and performance and show how the acquisition and development of schemas can account for some of the phenomena involved. But for now, let's see what the phenomena are: first, skilled performance without understanding, then understanding without skilled performance, and finally, some general phenomena.

There are situations in which good performance does not derive from understanding. Idiot savants are people who have spent their lifetimes practicing the mechanics of memory or of computation. But by definition, they are quite unexceptional (or even retarded) when it comes to the normal activities of daily living. They know the rules of computation, and they know large numbers of facts, but they do not have a deep understanding of what they do. Nevertheless, their performance is remarkable. Ask the right type of question and receive an instant reply:

Question: What is the square root of 529,374?

Reply: Let's see, 727.5, um, 8, 1—how many decimal places do you want?

Along these same lines, consider the way some people can parrot back facts and figures of history or formulas of mathematics with little comprehension beyond that necessary to apply them to a steryotyped situation. "There are three basic laws of electronics," an experienced electronics technician once reported to me. "One: ohms equals volts divided by amps; two: amps equals volts divided by ohms; three: volts equals ohms times amps." The Navy had taught him, he proudly announced, and he had been commanded to memorize all three! Performance and understanding are different things.

The complement of performance without understanding is understanding without performance. It isn't enough to know something. That knowledge must be available at the proper time. Moreover, it must be represented in a form appropriate to the specific needs of the moment. Consider three simple statements, each illustrating a different aspect of the relationship between knowledge and performance.

While scuba diving: If you get into trouble, release your weight belt.

While piloting an airplane: In the final approach to an airport prior to landing, lower the plane's landing gear.

While driving to work: When you pass the mailbox, mail these letters.

Three different statements, three different situations. Each contains a prescription for action that is easily learned, easily encoded into memory. "What have you just learned?" a teacher asks, and without much effort a rule can be restated. These are examples of what I call condition–action schemas. That is, a schema for such situations would be set up in the form, "Whenever the condition is satisfied, do the action."

But failures of performance occur despite relevant knowledge. Scuba divers have drowned close to shore with no apparent sign of trouble (they probably were exhausted or cold). In many of these cases all their equipment was intact and in perfect working order, but their weight belts were still in place: 15–20 pounds of lead were still fastened around their waists. The victims might not have drowned if only they had released their weights, an action that they must have known, for it is taught and emphasized in all diving classes. (This opinion is buttressed by reports of those who have survived.)

Airplane pilots sometimes attempt to land without lowering their landing gear (usually they receive a last-minute urgent call from the landing tower or copilot, but sometimes they complete the landing—a crash landing). Why didn't they do as they had been taught?

And what about mailing those letters? How many times have you returned home and gone through some version of, "Did I mail the letters? Oh, no, those letters!"

All three cases are examples of knowledge without action. In all of them the participants had their knowledge safely tucked away in a form that did not guarantee its application when it was relevant. Note the anomaly of remembering now what was forgotten then. Yet the memory system is unchanged. In all three examples the failure of performance resulted from a failure to retrieve, not from a lack of knowledge.

There are other ways to fail. Sometimes poor performance occurs even though the necessary knowledge is there and is being applied. In fact, poor performance may result from paying too much attention to the application of the relevant information.

Imagine a game of tennis. Think about how to hit your tennis ball. Consider your grip, the angle of the racket, the trajectory of the swing. Keep your elbow in proper position, watch those wrists. Now, keeping track of all the important conditions, watch the ball, compensate for the spin, for the type of playing surface (remembering that depression near the net), for the wind. Don't hit toward your opponent's backhand—okay, return that serve. How well would you have done in a real game? You would not have done well at all, I guarantee, for there is no better way to ruin performance than to think simultaneously about the details of its execution.

It is a common belief that the human mind excels in reasoning, is thought capable of determining appropriate courses of action when presented with a situation. What could be a more impressive sign of intellect than deep, reasoned thought—turning the mind this way and that, probing alternatives, consciously examining possible courses of action? The belief is overrated. Conscious thought is slow, serial, pedestrian, and severely constrained by a limited working memory.

Skilled performers do not need to concentrate on their actions. They have learned their skills so well that they can perform with a minimum amount of conscious attention to the task. Their performance seems automatic. The beginner struggles, concentrating on the task. Ask a beginner a question and the result can be a severe disruption of both the task and the answer. The beginning driver feels that driving an automobile requires more skills than one person can manage. The expert driver rarely feels taxed.

Skilled typists, merrily banging out 100 words a minute, can talk with you while typing. Skilled professional pianists speak of learning a piece "in the fingers" so well that if their minds take flight, their fingers continue playing without hesitation, sometimes to the surprise of the pianist. "I lost my place during a concert and had to listen to what I was playing until I could recognize where I was," a professional musician once told me.

Walking and talking are two of the most complicated tasks people do, each requiring skills that are still not understood by science. No machine can yet walk on two legs in the same manner as a human, let alone jump or hop or dance. No machine can speak or understand in a natural manner (despite some very real accomplishments in these areas in recent years). Yet people walk and talk; we can even do both at the same time. Our talking and walking usually happen automatically. (People who pace while thinking, however, are apt to stand still when their thoughts become complex.) For some people, word production is so independent of conscious thought that at times they are surprised by what they have written or said. I have even been known to stop lecturing when I hear myself say something interesting and write notes on my own lecture.

People seem to keep improving indefinitely as they practice a task. The figure shows one of the classic studies: cigar makers. Compare the beginning cigar maker (who has produced a mere 10,000 cigars) with one who has produced 100,000 or 1 million or 10 million. The speed of producing the cigars increases with the length of time the worker has been doing the task. In this particular study different people are being compared across a 10-year span of experience (see Figure 13-1).

What about doing simple arithmetic? We are all practiced at it, and sums come automatically to mind. Give yourself some concentrated practice, per-

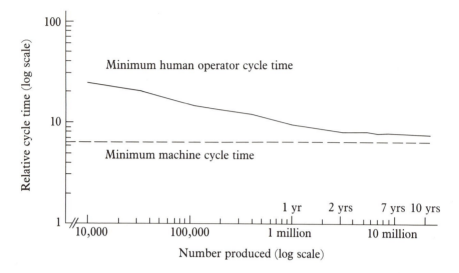

Figure 13-1.
This figure shows the continual improvement in the rate of making cigars by operators with different amounts of experience; even after approximately 10 years of experience and perhaps 20 million cigars, there is still some slight improvement noted. [After a study by Crossman (1959).]

haps doing another 10,000 sums, and watch your improvement. (See Figure 13-2). Practice at a reaction-time task: a pattern of 10 lights comes on, and as rapidly as possible you must depress the same pattern on 10 keys with your fingers. (Each finger is over one key, and the hand is held in a comfortable position.) With 10 lights there are 1023 possible patterns. Practice makes a person faster, at least for the first 75,000 trials (at which point the experimenter and the learner gave up).

In the laboratory it is difficult to study an expert's learning. What can you measure? What distinguishes the performance of top professionals from that of average professionals? Compare an airline pilot who has over 30 years' flying experience and 40,000 to 50,000 hours of flying time with a good pilot

---

Figure 13-2 (opposite).
Continued improvement in performance can be observed even after considerable (heroic) amounts of practice. Part A shows the results of a study by Blackburn (1936) in which the time that two different people took to perform mental additions continued to improve even after approximately 10,000 trials. Part B shows an experiment by Seibel (1963), which demonstrated continued improvement in speed of pressing combinations of 10 keys (1,023 alternatives) even after 75,000 trials. [Figures were adapted from Fitts (1964).]

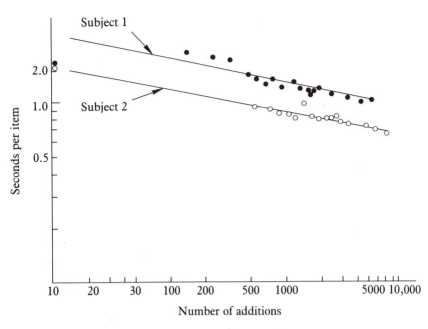

A

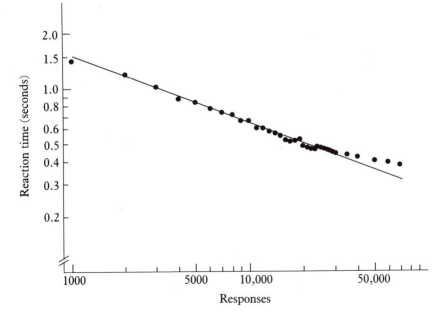

B

who has 300 hours of flying time. Compare the tennis champions with the best local players. How do we characterize the differences? If we could measure every aspect of the performance of pilots or pianists or tennis players, what would we make of the differences between expert and average? Studies have been made. Reels of video tape, computer tape, and motion-picture film, and numerous physiological measurements have been taken. We do know that the better performers are more skilled, but we don't know how to characterize the differences. The best pilots, for example, claim they become a "part" of the aircraft, anticipating, "flying ahead of the plane." Poorer pilots "keep their heads in the cockpit." How do we build a science from such observations? The research has a long way to go.

Expert performance is distinguished from very good performance in several ways. Five major characteristics have been examined by those who study skills: 1. smoothness, 2. automaticity, 3. mental effort, 4. performance under stress, and 5. point of view. The five characteristics are not independent; indeed, I suspect that when psychologists finally come to understand the nature of learning and performance, it will turn out that all five are the result of one common set of processes.

1. *Smoothness.* Smoothness is the apparent ease with which a professional performs. The professional seems to have time and goes gracefully and smoothly from one action to another. Watch a good amateur and a good professional at a sport, and it sometimes seems that the amateur is faster, more active. It is the amateur who makes the dramatic lunge, who works harder. The professional moves more slowly, and often does not seem to be doing anything special at all. The professional can make a task seem so easy that the unwary spectator may decide that it is the amateur who is superior.

2. *Automaticity.* As skill develops, a task appears to be done with more smoothness, with less effort. Moreover, as I have discussed, the expert often does the task automatically, without conscious awareness of exactly what has been done. Ask skilled typists how they type a space. Do they always use the same thumb or do they alternate thumbs according to the particular words they are typing? Many typists do not know what they do. They have to answer the question by mentally simulating typing and "observing" how they use the space bar. (Most skilled typists always type the space bar with the same thumb, usually the right one, but many of them think they use both thumbs.)

3. *Mental effort.* As skill increases, mental effort decreases. The task appears easier, there is less mental fatigue, less need to monitor

each action with care. Skilled performers can hold conversations with others, even while performing intricate tasks with their bodies. Mental resources seem limited, however, as if there were only a small pool available for use. Only so much conscious attention can be devoted to any one task at any one time. The limit on primary memory poses severe constraints on performance. There is an entire field of psychology—selective attention—devoted to the study of such limits. But when people become so skilled that performance becomes automated, the demands on conscious resources diminish. And with that lessening of demand comes a reduction in the apparent mental work load, a reduction in the apparent mental effort that is required (and a concomitant reduction in the mental fatigue following the completion of the task).

4. *Stress.* Stress quickly distinguishes the amateur from the expert. Stress robs a person of mental resources, and performance deteriorates. Skills that need few resources, skills that are automated, do not deteriorate as much under stress as skills less well practiced. The reason is not known, but probably has to do with automated behavior coupled with diminished mental effort. There are mental resources to spare. The responses to a stressful situation may already have been learned, practiced, and perhaps even made automatic.

5. *Point of view.* When you walk, you don't think about the placement of your legs but of where you wish to go. Flying an airplane or driving an automobile is done in that same way by the skilled performer. When you learned to drive, you concentrated on how to move your arms and legs. Then you worried about the smoothness of your activities. Eventually you reached the point where you simply thought of turning and your actions took care of themselves. But even that phase changed. The skilled driver simply goes somewhere—to the store, home, to the bank. The skilled walker decides to go to the other side of the room. The skilled airplane pilot no longer manipulates controls and watches instruments, but simply flies—not "flies the plane," but "flies." The person is flying or driving or going. The plane or the automobile or the legs are incidental tools to the activity.

14

Missionaries and Cannibals

Let me demonstrate the stages of learning and performance. I would like you to try a learning experiment that will take approximately 30 minutes. You will need six objects to manipulate: three large, three small. I use large and small paper clips. You will also need paper, a pencil, and a way of measuring time in seconds.

I want you to solve the missionaries and cannibals problem described on page 76. Then I want you to learn the solution. Practice it over and over until you can do the task in less than 10 seconds. I mean actually do the task: move the paper clips back and forth. (If you are familiar with the problem, read it anyway—I have modified it.) Continue reading only after you have read the box and done the missionary-cannibal task according to the criterion.

The solution to the problem is shown below. It can be thought of as taking 11 moves, divided into three phases:

    I. Get all the missionaries over to the other side.

   II. Get all the cannibals over to the other side.

  III. Clean up: in the process of doing phase II, some of the missionaries must go back to the original side of the river.

Although phases I and III are straightforward, phase II is not. Move 6 causes a retreat from the goal. Most people have difficulty with move 6 because it is contrary to intuition. See Figure 14-1.

The paper-clip version of the missionaries and cannibals problem has the convenient property of letting you transform yourself from a hesitant, stumbling novice into a smooth, skillful expert in relatively little time. Let's examine what happens as the task is repeated over and over again. What changes take place in your knowledge?

Note that as you continue to practice the solution, you are not learning much about how to solve the problem, but you are learning a lot about how to *perform*. As you progress, your representation of the task changes from deduction or problem solving to memory to motor skill. As you practice more and more, your actions become smoother and more automatic. At first you struggle to complete the task in 30 seconds. Then you occasionally do it in 10. Eventually you will always finish in 7 or 8, with occasional times as low as 5 seconds.

Learning this simple task takes much more time than most people expect. I have found it may take an hour or more. And the skill must be practiced or it will deteriorate. Even though I have done the task many times, I find I must practice half an hour each year, just before I present the problem to my students; otherwise I chance getting confused in class.

The task is useful for exploring various aspects of learning. To see another change that comes with practice, you might try reversing the situation at some point in your learning (or in a friend's). This time suppose the cannibals are not to outnumber the missionaries, who might then risk being eaten. The reversal usually has different effects at different stages of learning. Near the beginning, it has almost no effect because the original task has not been well enough learned for a change to make any noticeable difference. If reversal is made after considerable skill has been acquired, it makes little difference because the general pattern of the solution is unchanged. But if the situation is reversed at a midway point—when the solution times are about 15 seconds—the change leads to major difficulty.

In Chapter 13 I listed five characteristics of skilled performance: smoothness, automaticity, mental effort, performance under stress, and point of view. You can see each of these characteristics in your own performance on the missionaries and cannibals problem.

Smoothness is probably one of the more apparent elements of skilled performance. When you first started the task, it is likely that you were hesitant and made many false starts, many errors. The paper clips slipped or bumped into each other, making it difficult to keep track of where you were. The physical manipulation of the objects interfered with performance. But as you improved, the performance became smoother; disruptions and false starts were eliminated.

With sufficient practice, the movement of the paper clips becomes auto-

The Missionaries and Cannibals Problem

Three missionaries were lost, exploring the jungles of the planet Aurilion. Separated from their companions, without food or radio, they knew only that their destination was ahead. They stood at a river that blocked their path, wondering what to do. All at once, three cannibals appeared, carrying with them a boat. They too were about to cross the river. Groups of cannibals and missionaries had met before. Each was respectful of the other, but not fully trusting; missionaries took advantage of cannibals whenever they outnumbered them, and the unwitting cannibals were baptized before they could escape.

The three cannibals were willing to help the missionaries cross the river, but their boat could hold only two people at a time, and the cannibals would not let themselves ever be outnumbered by the missionaries. How can the problem be solved?

The Task

Your task is to manipulate the paper clips back and forth across the river: let large clips represent missionaries and small ones cannibals. You must imagine the boat. Remember that the boat holds a maximum of two people at a time. If on one side of the river there are ever more missionaries than cannibals, you have failed and must start over. Remember to count whoever is in the boat, so that one missionary and one cannibal on the river bank plus one or two missionaries in the boat at the same side of the river spells trouble.

matic, requiring little or no conscious thought or control. Full automaticity requires a considerable amount of practice—more than the 30 minutes or so that most people are willing to spend on this task. But even if you spent only 15 minutes manipulating the paper clips, you probably could feel some of the moves becoming automatic. Ultimately you can learn to do the task entirely in your mind, without external props. First you can do it without using paper clips, by just moving your hand. Later on you stop moving your hand.

Mental work load decreases as you practice. In the initial stages of doing the problem, there was a reasonably heavy mental work load. At first, this burden was computational: you had to think through the solution each time. If someone had asked you a question midway through the task, it would have been disruptive. Then the burden changed to being a load on primary memory. You were attempting to remember the solution, not to rederive it each

Try it. Move the paper clips back and forth. Expect to take as long as 10 minutes to solve it the first time.

Time each attack on the problem. If you err in any manner (dropping a paper clip, moving the wrong clip by mistake, or finding a baptized cannibal), you must start the problem over but without stopping the timing. The time for the task must include all your actions from the start to a successful completion.

Write down the time for each trial on a piece of paper. Keep at the task until you can do it twice in a row in less than 10 seconds each time.

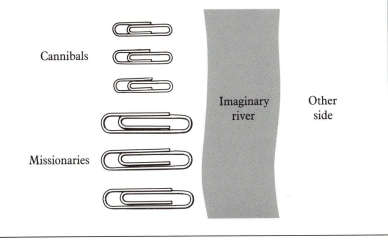

Cannibals

Missionaries

Imaginary river

Other side

time. Later on the memory burden became greatly reduced—almost completely eliminated, in fact.

Stress is perhaps the hardest point to illustrate. (The missionaries and cannibals problem is hardly a matter of life and death.) Perhaps you could assemble an audience and announce that you were going to solve the problem in exactly 10 seconds, on your first attempt. Wager money on it (or better yet, pride). If you make the wager too soon, you are apt to fail, because the stress of the public performance is likely to take its toll. I know. After becoming an expert at home, I foolishly made such a statement in my classroom, only to be met with clumsy fingers and recalcitrant paper clips.

Point of view shifts as you master the solution. When you started the missionaries and cannibals problem, you concentrated on remembering (or deducing) the moves. With practice the focus of attention changed. If you kept at it long enough, you reached the point where you could watch your hands perform the task as you thought ahead about the next set of actions. The description of the problem changes. As you get better and better, you no longer view the problem as one involving missionaries and cannibals, which is the description given by the 11 steps of the solution; rather, you see the problem as a sequence of operations. For example, when I do the task I concentrate solely on the action (how many people are in the boat), and so to me the moves look like those shown in Figure 14-1B.

The missionaries and cannibals problem lets you get the feel of the differences among the stages of learning as you progress from being a novice to being an expert in a reasonably short period. But a description of the differences in performance is not enough. What is needed is a theory of learning and performance, a theory that can conceptualize the process of learning.

For years I have followed an elusive trail, seeking better understanding of the nature of human learning. I seek an explanation of the learning process. I want to know what psychological mechanisms are involved, what knowledge structures are formed. I want the theory to specify the internal operations of mental processes, the organization of information within memory, and the changes that take place during the process of learning. How can one conceptualize the learning process?

Chaos, analysis, synthesis, automatization—these are terms the psychologist Robert S. Woodworth used in 1938 to describe the progress of a person taking part in an elaborate experiment in learning. I like his characterization of the learning process. It accords well with my own experiences in learning new, complicated activities. Think back to the missionaries and cannibals problem, or to when you first learned to drive a car, to type, or to play a musical instrument. The sequence proceeds from whole to part and back to whole again. At first the task is chaotic—unorganized. Not enough is known even to perceive the situation easily. Then, with more experience, some of the units emerge. Systematic analysis reveals the component parts, which can then be learned separately, interrelated, and combined. Larger organizational units emerge; the topic takes on some structure and finally seems to

---

Figure 14-1.
The solution to the missionaries and cannibals problem is shown in A: a sequence of 11 actions. As an expert, my conceptualization is changed: I divide the task into the three phases shown in B. Note that the only part of the task that concerns me is the action: Who is in the boat? In what direction is the boat moving? Having learned these 11 actions, I can perform the task without error, with great speed. But I also no longer keep track of why I do each act. In some sense, I no longer understand what I am doing, even though I am an expert at the task, and this sequence could be arrived at only after complete understanding. But mindless performance of an action sequence is sometimes superior performance of that action. [After Woodworth (1938).]

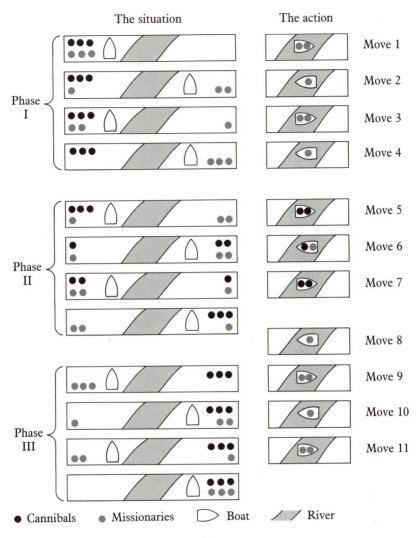

The situation   The action

Phase I — Move 1, Move 2, Move 3, Move 4

Phase II — Move 5, Move 6, Move 7, Move 8

Phase III — Move 9, Move 10, Move 11

● Cannibals   ● Missionaries   ⬡ Boat   ▨ River

A

Phase I	Phase II	Phase III
1	5	8
2	6	9
3	7	10
4		11

B

be manageable. With further experience, the use of the knowledge becomes automatic, the skilled performance becomes subconscious.

The different stages of the learning cycle also correspond to different activities in the construction of mental representations of the knowledge being acquired. At the least, learning consists simply of the entering of new information into memory. At the most, learning consists of a dramatic reconceptualization of knowledge, with important new conceptual structures being acquired for the first time. In addition, some learning consists of an improved conception of already existing knowledge. Practicing tennis serves is not likely to add new conceptualizations to memory, nor can it be characterized as a major acquisition of new information into memory. But because practice will improve performance, something has indeed been learned.

The role of the past in the perception and identification of objects and events is another concept that is continually rediscovered in psychology. Although this concept of recognition requires that what is being experienced be labeled as an example of something experienced earlier, it is surprisingly difficult to realize that this demand puts a heavy burden on one's past knowledge and experiences. It means that everything is identified as an instance of something else, further specified to mark the distinctions and special characteristics of the present experience. If perceptual events are identified in terms of prior knowledge, then how is it possible to learn anything new? One answer is that there are three main ways of doing so, three modes of learning.

15

Accretion, Structuring, Tuning: Modes of Learning

My colleague David Rumelhart and I have found it useful to categorize the several aspects of learning into these three modes:

1. *Accretion*. Accretion is the addition of new knowledge to existing memory schemas. The framework exists, but new data are entered. Accretion is the most common mode of learning.

2. *Structuring*. Structuring is the formation of new conceptual structures, of new conceptualizations. The existing schemas will no longer suffice; new schemas must be formed. The structuring mode occurs infrequently and usually entails great effort and struggle. But structuring is probably the most important of the modes.

3. *Tuning*. Tuning is the fine adjustment of knowledge to a task. The proper schemas exist and appropriate knowledge is within them. But they are inefficient for the purpose, either because they are too general or because they are mismatched to the particular use that is required of them, so the knowledge must be tuned, continually adjusted to the task. Practice is one way of accomplishing tuning. It may take thousands of hours of practice to reach the stage of tuning that characterizes an expert. Tuning

is perhaps the slowest of the modes of learning, but it is what changes mere knowledge of a topic into expert performance.

Accretion is the process of gradual accumulation of knowledge. In the best of circumstances the new knowledge fits within a prior framework of knowledge that is appropriate for organizing and maintaining the information, as in Figure 15-1. In other circumstances the fit is bad, and the newly acquired knowledge is apt to be tucked away into inaccessible areas of memory or interpreted in inappropriate ways. Accretion is the form of learning that you (a skilled driver) engage in when you start to drive a new automobile. Presumably you already have a good framework of knowledge for the structure of automobiles and for the mechanics of driving. Still, you must learn the specific details of a new car—where the horn and the emergency brake are located, how much free play the steering wheel has, and how tight the brakes are. Basically, as you come across each new aspect of the car, you are able to tuck it away in memory in some well-established manner. The problem of learning becomes a problem of memory acquisition and retrieval.

Start with structuring; I wish to show you two very nice experimental results. Unfortunately, both results are suspect and neither one is in current favor in psychology. Even so, I believe them. Let me explain.

One of these experiments is a study done in the late 1890s on the learning of Morse code; the other experiment is a study done in 1910 on the learning of wire puzzles. Both illustrate the jump in knowledge that occurs in the process of learning. Consider the graph in Figure 15-2.

The graph shows the speed at which learners could transmit and receive Morse code as a function of the amount of training. Note the plateaus in the curves. There is a slow, gradual improvement in performance (attributable to what I would call accretion), followed by a long plateau of little or no improvement. Occasionally there are spurts of learning, abrupt jumps in the learning curve. I attribute the jumps to the process of restructuring the problem, learning anew with more appropriate memory structures. I believe that in many different learning situations there are stages of progress, with sudden breakthroughs in understanding that lead to spurts in performance.

The curves in the graph mirror my own youthful experience in learning Morse code. For a long time my rate of receiving hovered around 15 words a minute, and I seemed unable to improve it. That rate was too slow to keep up with the experienced operators I was hearing.

One day, a neighbor took me to visit an ancient veteran of Morse code, a professional, a person whose livelihood had depended on his ability to send and receive with accuracy, at speeds of about 60 words a minute. He leaned back in his chair, whiskey glass in hand, and told me that I was doing the wrong task. I was receiving letters, when I should really be receiving messages, or at least words and phrases. "Don't receive the word *this* as the separate letters *t-h-i-s*," he told me. "Learn instead the pattern of sounds for the whole word. Learn the patterns for common letter sequences, then learn the patterns for common words, then common phrases." He proceeded to demonstrate by turning on his radio and finding a code station. Then, while still talking to me, he would pause every so often to tell me what had just been transmitted.

I went home and practiced words, and my receiving speed took a dramatic spurt upward. What I had learned from the friendly old telegrapher was to restructure my conceptualization of the task. I had to change the level of the units I was working with. I was probably told to do that at just the right time; I already had a solid base of performance on the individual letters, and so I was able to benefit from the advice to enlarge the unit size—to restructure my knowledge. Bryan and Harter, who presented the results shown in the graph, put it this way: "A plateau in the learning curve means that the lower-order habits are approaching their maximum development, but are not yet sufficiently automatic to leave the attention free to attack the higher-order habits."

In these terms, I had developed the lower-order habits but had not realized that I should progress to higher orders. Once I restructured my habits improvement followed.

All is not well with Bryan and Harter, however. They may have been a bit free with their data, and their results do not stand up under careful scrutiny. The psychologist Fred Keller, a careful experimenter and also a skilled telegrapher and teacher of telegraphy, reports that he has been completely unable to repeat Bryan and Harter's findings. In a classic paper titled "The Phantom Plateau," Keller reported that he not only failed to find plateaus of development among his students, but that he could find no real evidence that Bryan and Harter found any either. Their "data" are not data of the sort you collect in the laboratory. They are reports, after the fact, of what the telegraphers thought had happened to them.

Keller makes a strong case, but he cannot shake my faith in the basic phenomenon. I believe that there are different levels of learning and that there is a reconceptualization of the task on the part of the learner. I believe that as we gain new insight into a topic, performance significantly changes. It is a belief that seems too powerful and too commonplace to be denied. Many skills seem to go through plateaus or even regressions in performance as we attempt to reorganize the manner in which they are performed—ultimately for the better, but initially only with great difficulty and sometimes with a slight decrement in performance. Keller also believes that changes in the unit size occur in the learning of Morse code. But he believes they occur simultaneously with the learning of the lower-level units, that the learning of phrases and words in code occurs simultaneously with the learning of indi-

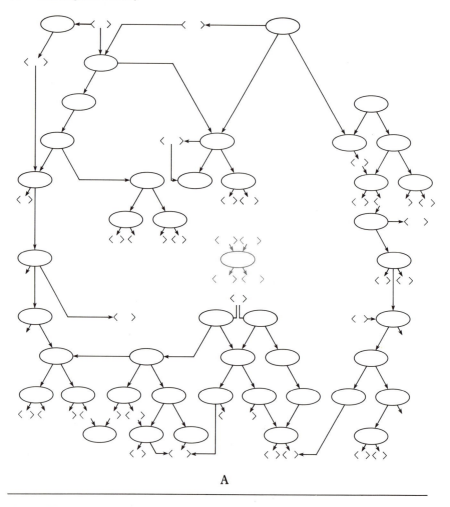

A

Figure 15-1.
*Suppose the stuff in part A is the knowledge structure for some topic. At the center, a
small unit of new knowledge is about to be inserted (accreted) into the existing structures.
And in B, the accretion is complete, with enough new bonds established among the new
and old structures so that the two are firmly intermeshed, with no discontinuities: learning
at its best.*

vidual letters. The result is a smooth, ever-increasing improvement in learning ability. He may be right—but his belief contradicts my remembrance of
my own performance. Of course, my remembrance may be as faulty as the
data reported by Bryan and Harter. As studies of memory repeatedly show,
the remembrance of things long past is often closer to what we imagine them
to have been than to what they really were.

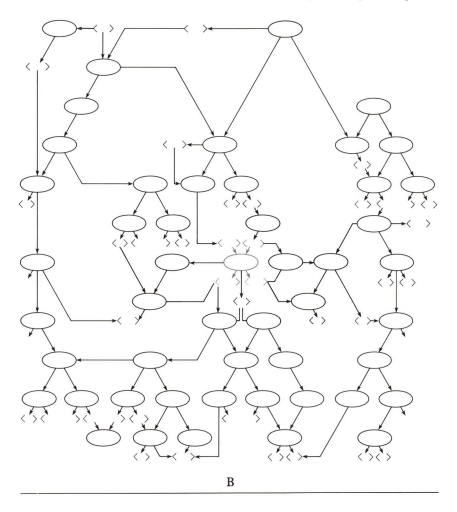

B

My other favorite graph depicts the amount of time taken to solve a mechanical wire puzzle as a function of the number of attempts. You are probably familiar with such puzzles. There are usually two parts (each a piece of wire bent into a clever pattern), which are intertwined. The object is to get them apart, a task that would appear hopeless except that you know the puzzle can be solved (Figure 15-3). I have not been able to figure out exactly what puzzle was used in the study (the author calls it "star and crescent"), but it really doesn't matter.

The data were initially reported in 1910. The significant point is, of course, what happened at about trial 75, where the puzzle solver stopped, thought deeply about the problem, and essentially said, "Aha, now I have it!" Prior to trial 75, the solver had been doing relatively well, but there was no understanding of the problem. If the solver moved the puzzle in a certain way, well, it came apart. But once the principle was understood, on that special trial, then performance improved by becoming more consistent; the variability in solution times was reduced (Figure 15-3B).

I call the long solution time an illustration of the structuring process. What is wrong with the data? Nothing really, but the paper in which the results were reported leaves me uneasy. It is too casual, too informal. I wonder about what was happening, what the person was told to do, how representative the curve is. Still, there is something to the sudden change in knowledge. In fact, in my own experiments I have been able to create similar sudden changes.

I have been studying how people learn a simple programming language. (The language is called FLOW.) Among the many variations I have tried is one in which I make the instructional text deliberately confusing. Take the following statement, read rather early by a student who was starting to learn the commands of the language:

The *G* statement moves the current value one position to the right in the input data.

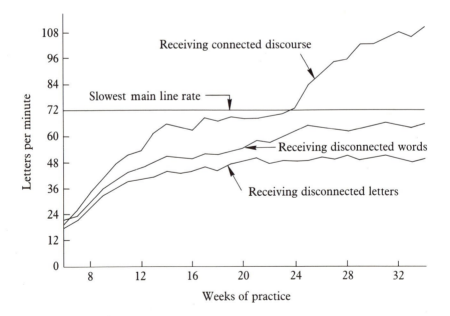

Figure 15-2.
The data are from the studies of the learning of American Morse code, conducted by Bryan and Harter (1897, 1899). These are classic curves for demonstrating the existence of learning plateaus, the flat areas reflect periods of relatively little learning.

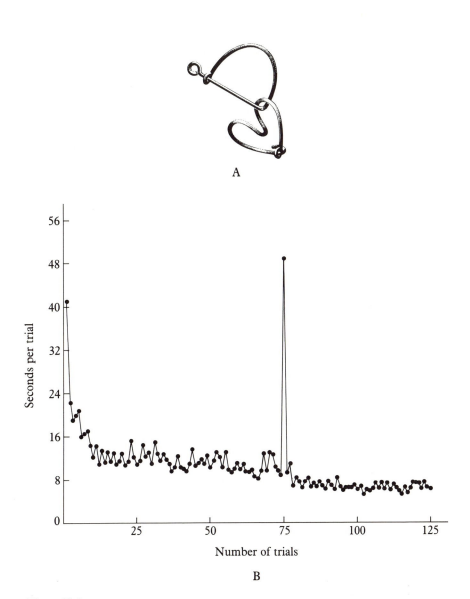

A

B

Number of trials

Figure 15-3.
The effect of practice is reflected in the amount of time required to solve a mechanical puzzle, of the sort shown in part A. The data in part B are from an experiment by Ruger (1910). Although the subject solved the puzzle on every trial, on trial 75 there was a long period of reflection, followed by even improved performance, the major change being a reduction in the variability of solution times from trial to trial. [From Experimental Psychology by R.S. Woodworth. Copyright © 1938 by Holt, Rinehart and Winston, Inc. Reprinted by permission of Holt, Rinehart and Winston, CBS College Publishing.]

Is the statement obscure? I worked hard to make it so. I labeled the statement by a letter (*G*) instead of a mnemonic name (the actual programming language used the name "Get input value"), and I shortened the description, using as much jargon as possible.

Students typically read the statement and uncomprehendingly passed right over it. Later, when they needed it for a problem they were working on, I would point to the part of the instruction where the statement appeared and ask them to read it again. "Oh, I see," they would say, and that was that.

Most of us have had similar experiences. The instruction manual for a new device is often obscure at first. Sometimes we have to read the manual four or five times in the course of learning, each time getting something new out of it. Often the new learning is preceded by a critical state of confusion, for we must be ready to use the information we seek. Only then is the relevant material interpretable.

Here is how one of the students in my experiment put it. She had been working at learning the programming system, and she was unable to solve a particularly complex problem. I showed her the page of the instruction manual that discussed the relevant instruction. She read it, said "Of course!" and immediately corrected her program. Later, she was asked to explain what had happened.

Student: I was dumbfounded. I would look at the screen, and all the things I had been working with all day and all week meant nothing to me. Umm. Then I read the paragraph in the manual on FLOW and everything just came to me in a snap.

Experimenter: But you had read that paragraph before.

Student: Yes, yes, I had read it and all of a sudden . . .

Experimenter: But if you had read it before why didn't you remember it?

Student: I don't know. I guess because I had been . . . Well, I was confused. I'd been reading different things all day, maybe, umm, well, I wasn't thinking in that train of thought, of the umm, of the VALUE. I was thinking about TEXT. And I guess I didn't relate the two until I read that paragraph.

The special state of sudden insight seems fundamentally important to the learning process. It seems to require a critical state of confusion on the part of the student and the proper presentation of instruction at just the right moment. The restructuring of knowledge is an infrequent occurrence, but when it occurs, it leads to fundamental improvements in understanding. (Note too the link with the retrieval specifications discussed earlier. The student had the relevant information in memory, but her description was inappropriate.)

As already noted, when skill develops, a task appears to be done with more smoothness, with less effort. Moreover, the expert appears to do the task automatically, without mental effort, without conscious awareness of what has been done. The change that occurs in transforming a person knowledgeable about the task into one who is expert is the mode of learning Rumelhart and I named tuning. Tuning is the slow, continual adjustment in the knowledge structures of the performer to make them more efficient, more specialized, more automatic—to make them tuned specifically to the demands of the task.

When something becomes automated, what happens? How can a knowledge structure that already seems sufficient and complete become more efficient? Computer programmers will recognize that there are major differences in the efficiency of different programs, even though each does exactly the same task; a major difference can be found in the contrast between a program written for an interpretive language and one that has been compiled into a machine language. Another approach is to think of the difference between knowledge about something and knowledge of how to do something (declarative versus procedural knowledge) or of the difference between general knowledge and specific knowledge. General knowledge allows one to deduce all sorts of things, but at the cost of speed and of effort in computation. Specific knowledge lacks generality, but it is efficient for the task. Thus I can multiply by virtue of knowing that multiplication is repeated addition, but multiplying in that way is slow and requires much effort. I can also multiply by memorizing the specific products of frequently encountered numbers; that requires a lot of effort initially, and a lot of memory space, but when I need an answer, it comes fast, without much mental effort.

What is tuning? It might be the development of specific knowledge for specific cases, requiring much memory storage but resulting in efficient performance. Tuning might be the compilation of commonly used actions into an efficient code for performing those actions. It might be moving the level of the knowledge to states below those that require conscious attention. Tuning might be all of these—and other things as well. Whatever it is, it is an essential phase of learning.

Accretion, structuring, and tuning seem to be three basic modes of progression from being a novice to being a skilled performer. What is it exactly that takes place during these stages of learning? Alas, the answers are not known, but the search has begun. Several promising lines of research are being followed by investigators around the world. Today I can tell you no more than yesterday's results, results that now seem incomplete without next year's promises. That is the way of research, with the topic of today demanding full attention, holding out for the future the heady promise of complete understanding.

16

Learning
as Story Understanding

They pushed us into a large white room and my eyes
began to blink because the light hurt them.

Jean-Paul Sartre, "The Wall"

That sentence is the opening line of a story by Jean-Paul Sartre. Stop for a moment, close your eyes and think about the implications of the sentence. What you did in attempting to understand it provides an example of the mental activity that accompanies the understanding of new material. You must determine the point of the sentence and construct a mental scenario of the situation, the better to incorporate the events that will be revealed as the story develops. Following a story or a poem—or just the daily events of life—requires the development of a consistent framework for relating the different aspects of knowledge. The task in understanding a new situation is, in part, to find existing schemas from past knowledge that can act as a guide to the development of an appropriate new schema for the current situation.

In life, the events in which we participate usually flow smoothly. There is continuity to the events, and present activities are good predictors of future expectations. As we travel from place to place through the day, new events seldom thrust themselves on us unexpectedly. Even as we approach new places, we have strong expectations of the general flow of events. Obviously there are times when the unexpected does occur, but, with the exception of the very exceptional, even unexpected occurrences are constrained to be consistent with the existing situation. Suppose you are at work in your office when a colleague walks in with two cups of coffee. The act is a surprise, yes, but it is consistent with the activities of the office. What about walking down the street and being unexpectedly hit in the back by a child's ball? It can take a moment to figure out what happened. The act is a surprise, but it is consistent with the earlier sight or sound of children playing and with the normal activities that take place on that street. In such cases there can be a moment when there is no interpretation, sometimes followed by an erroneous interpretation ("I've been hit by a car"), but it usually does not take long for the correct interpretation to occur.

In general we can base our expectations of the world's events on our past knowledge and the easy transition from one activity to another. There are certain situations, however, in which the smooth analysis of events is disrupted. One such situation is illustrated by the opening line of this chapter. The skillful novelist or dramatist deliberately selects the information to be revealed to the reader or viewer, parceling out just enough clues to keep the audience in whatever state of confusion or expectancy is desired. Another situation is the case of learning or experiencing something new, in which the experience becomes one of continual attempts to understand in terms of what is known. When we are trying to learn, we must develop new, appropriate schemas that can be used to guide performance.

Reconsider the quotation from Sartre. The sentence by itself describes a reasonably straightforward situation. "We" (that is, "I," the narrator of the story, along with some other people) have been pushed by unspecified persons into a large white room. The light, either sunlight or artificial light, hurt my eyes and caused me to blink. Readers are expected to go far beyond these simple statements. The word "pushed" implies "against our will." Large white rooms are not all that common, and the normal reader will construct a scenario around the situations in which such rooms could occur, together with the implications of "pushed." One possibility is that it is a hospital recovery room or an operating room. Maybe it's an interrogation room at a police station: imagine the narrator, his hands bound behind his back, being thrust forward from a small, dark cage into the light by a sneering guard with a cigarette hanging from his lips. That mental schema more than accounts for the sentence. It sets up a structure with strong implications for the future development of the story. The skilled novelist expects you to construct a scenario and can deliberately cause you to misapprehend the events; an author can also build up suspense by controlling the sort of schemas you would normally construct.

A surprising thing about stories is how little information is needed in order to hit on an appropriate scenario. A novelist has considerable freedom in developing openings to a story, yet readers do not take long to zero in on an appropriate scenario. My colleague David Rumelhart has examined how readers do this with the sentences of Sartre's story. (Rumelhart modified the original story slightly to make its experimental analysis easier. Students saw the story one sentence at a time—and in some cases, one word at a time.

The first sentence was essentially as presented here, with minor changes in wording.) Rumelhart reported that the students developed a scenario (or a schema) consistent with what had so far been presented and with their own existing knowledge. Each successive sentence of the story expands on the developing schema and adds new information that constrains the interpretation. The reader of a story tends to go far beyond the information given, but if the tendency is to overinterpret, it is not done blindly. The reader knows that the decisions are tentative and that there may be a change in hypothesis as the story develops and new information arrives.

Let me illustrate the dynamic role of the development of hypothetical scenarios with an illustration from a different story. The first seven sentences of this eight-sentence "story" were constructed by Rumelhart out of the opening paragraph of the short story "Miss Brill" by Katherine Mansfield. (The eighth sentence was included to let the readers in the experiment figure out the story, if they had not already done so.) As you read each sentence of the story, pause and think about your impressions. In Rumelhart's experiment the people reading the story were asked to answer the following set of questions after reading each sentence:

Who do you see as characters in this story?

What do you think is happening in this story?

When do you think this story takes place?

Where do you think this story takes place?

Why do you think all this is happening?

(After each sentence I will prompt you with the list of questions: Who? What? When? Where? Why? Some questions will be inappropriate, but use them as a way to think about your own developing thoughts. As you read the story, cover up all the sentences except the one being read.)

1. Dear little thing.
   (*Who? What? When? Where? Why?*)

2. It was nice to feel it again.
   (*Who? What? When? Where? Why?*)

3. She had taken it out of its box that afternoon, given it a good brush and rubbed life back into the dim little eyes.
   (*Who? What? When? Where? Why?*)

4. Little rogue! Yes, she really felt that way about it.
   (*Who? What? When? Where? Why?*)

5. She put it on.
   (Who? What? When? Where? Why?)

6. Little rogue, biting its tail just by her left ear.
   (Who? What? When? Where? Why?)

7. When she breathed, something gentle seemed to move on her bosom.
   (Who? What? When? Where? Why?)

8. The day was cool and she was glad she had decided on her little fur.
   (Who? What? When? Where? Why?)

Rumelhart found that the answers to the What question fell into seven categories. The little rogue could be an item of clothing (shawl, hat, or jewelry). More specifically, it could be a piece of fur. Some people thought the opening sentence indicated a letter. Even the second sentence is consistent with the contents of a letter. Others thought the story was about a pet or a toy. Some people at first thought of the object in sexual terms. And some either did not form a concrete hypothesis or were unwilling to state it to the experimenter.

The figure shows the way three typical people varied in their hypotheses of what was happening. Each successive sentence added to the emerging picture. Sometimes the hypotheses were affected, sometimes not. But by the seventh sentence of this particular story, all three of the people had converged on the proper interpretation.

Story understanding is very much an active process. It requires the building of appropriate mental structures that are far more elaborate than a simple interpretation of the words of the sentences would warrant. Stories have purposes. Participants have motives. The storywriter is like a stage director, except that the set must be constructed within the reader's head, with only the bare cues provided by the writer. Good writers understand that, and often capitalize on the process. In some stories—short stories and mystery novels especially—they play games with the reader, subtly leading him or her to false conceptions and erroneous conclusions.

Magicians play on the same phenomenon with ease. James Randi, the magician who performs professionally as "The Amazing Randi," has written of the process:

It is the ability of the human mind to arrive at conclusions with an incomplete set of facts or insufficient sensory data that the magician uses to achieve some of his most potent illusions. Without such a facility, the human organism—in fact, any animal—would be unable

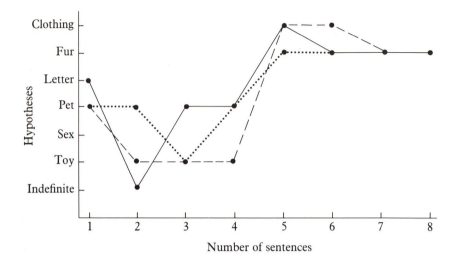

Figure 16-1.
Changing hypotheses about the topic of the story "Dear Little Thing" in the experiment performed by Rumelhart are shown here. Each line represents the path of a different person, and the major hypothesis held about the story at the conclusion of each successive sentence. Thus after the first sentence, two people thought the story to be about a pet, one thought the story to be about a letter.

After the second sentence, two of the readers changed their hypotheses, one now thought that it was about a toy, the other withheld judgment about the selection. At least one reader changed the current hypothesis with each new presentation of a sentence up to the seventh sentence, at which time all three readers had arrived at the correct hypothesis. (And if you consider that fur is a piece of clothing, so that both fur and clothing are correct, all three readers had developed the correct hypothesis by the fifth sentence.)

to function; for every moment, we make assumptions about our surroundings that are based upon flimsy evidence, bolstered by memories of past experience in similar circumstances and by the presumptions that the world is pretty much the way it was when we last tested it in this way.

(*Technology Review*, January 1978, p. 56.)

Randi points out, moreover, that the magician plants hypotheses, nourishes them, then demolishes them. By the skillful use of cues, the magician can guide the formation of false hypotheses and thereby control them.

The learner sometimes functions in much the same way as a story understander. The person reading a story puts together a cohesive account of the events described by the writer. The scenario is richly embellished, both by the past experience of the reader and by the unfolding of the various events described in the story. A person listening to a lecture or reading a text is in many ways like a person listening to a story, creating hypotheses that are sometimes valid, sometimes false.

17

The Teaching of Ed: A Case Study in Learning

For several years now my colleagues and I have sought to understand what goes on during the learning process. We have watched students whiz through topics or struggle for hours and finally give up. We have tried using a variety of teaching techniques: lecturing, coaching, tutoring. We imitated the teaching style of Socrates and of boring pedants. We asked students to behave normally or to think aloud. We paired up students and had them coach each other on their exercises. Sometimes we used study material taken from commercially available textbooks or instruction manuals and sometimes we prepared special material, including television tapes, instruction manuals, interactive sequences, and helpful hints.

One of our goals was to understand the learning process sufficiently well to be able to simulate it on a computer. That is, we wished to construct a computer program that would learn in the same way the people we had observed did, with the same types of difficulties, errors, and confusions. The task proved to be harder than we had imagined, and it has not yet been completed. Let me tell you a little about our philosophy and results, for the attempt was valuable in teaching us about learning and understanding. In fact, I think we learned more from our failures than we would have learned from success.

Psychologists have long studied the learning process, but they have a tendency to simplify the task to be learned until it is manageable and to choose tasks that will not last longer than an hour. My colleagues and I were afraid that basic properties of the learning process had been lost by such simplification. Therefore we looked for a real task that people actually learn, one that would take considerable time, but one that also seemed reasonable for experimental use. We started with studies of a wide variety of subjects: the history of the American Civil War; the psychology of the human auditory system; cooking (the French white sauces); computer programming; and even motor skills including juggling, unicycling, table tennis, and computer games such as Pong. We finally decided to concentrate on a task that exists in our own laboratory. We studied how people who knew nothing of computers learned to use a text editor, a computer program that lets the user make editorial changes in manuscripts (texts).

This book was written with the aid of a text editor. First the text material—a rough draft—was typed on a terminal, a typewriter that sends the appropriate electric signals to the computer for each character that is typed. Then, by giving the appropriate commands to the program, I could place separate chapters in separate computer files; find a chapter and look at selected portions; extract parts of a chapter and move them to other sections of the same or other chapters; correct misspelled words easily; change every occurrence of any particular word throughout the entire manuscript (with a single command); collect the references by searching my previous papers (and the papers of my students and colleagues that were also on the computer, with their permission) and transfer the desired ones to the book files.

The particular text editor available on our laboratory computer is called Ed. It is not easy to learn. Ed has many peculiar features, and it seems to be designed more to fit the idiosyncratic nature of the designer than the needs of a nonexpert user. But it is a real text editor used by thousands of people across the country, and because we wished to discover how people learn real tasks, we did not attempt to improve Ed. Real tasks usually have quirks, and the learner must come to understand their nature.

Here is a very brief introduction to Ed, a text editor. Basically, Ed is a computer program. It has a set of commands that it understands, and once a user has learned the fundamentals of Ed, it provides a useful method of writing any material in which there will be numerous changes. When a change must be made, only the information relevant to the change has to be entered into Ed; the whole manuscript does not need to be retyped.

My colleagues and I have found that it helps to think of Ed by analogy. Start by thinking of Ed as a secretary who types from your dictation. But Ed is a limited secretary. Ed believes exactly what it has been told, and orders are followed literally, without intelligence.

To write a letter with Ed, you would say, "Start a letter." Then everything you said would be added to the letter until you gave a contrary command. To continue dictating you would have to indicate where you were starting: "Add the following to the letter, starting at the second paragraph."

In fact, with Ed all commands must be given by typing them on the typewriter keyboard of the computer terminal. Typing causes a problem, because the commands and the text to be worked on look the same; the normal cues of voice intonation and inflection cannot be applied.

The computer terminal that we use is something like a combination of an electric typewriter and a television set. The user types on the keyboard section of the terminal, and responses from the computer are displayed on the television screen. Our screens can present 24 lines of print, with up to 80 characters on any line—the computer equivalent of a sheet of paper. It is more convenient than paper because a full 24 lines of text can be displayed in less than a second; it is less convenient because there is no permanent record of what has occurred.

The secretary analogy is useful in understanding the basic command structure of Ed. A card-file analogy is useful in understanding how the material is stored.

You can think of things in this way. Every line of text that you tell Ed to save is entered on a separate "file card," one line of text per card. The cards are kept in sequential order in a box that is called a buffer. If you wish to refer to any card, you can do so either by specifying what is on it (an advanced technique) or by specifying its numerical order in the sequence of cards, the technique used here. The number actually specifies the line number of the text, but you can think of it as the card number.

The commands all have the same basic format, $\# C<R>$, where $\#$ is the line number of the text. The line number can sometimes be given in the form *a,b,* which means the set of lines starting at line number *a* going up to and including line number *b*. C is the first letter of the name of the command, and $<R>$ means to type the key labeled RETURN on the keyboard. Typing $<R>$ is equivalent to typing the carriage return on an electric typewriter. Because of the way this computer system operates, Ed does not see anything being typed until $<R>$ has been typed, at which point it examines the entire line.

The three commands of interest are APPEND, PRINT, and DELETE. The APPEND command means that everything typed after the command should be added by Ed into the buffer. The process goes on until the STOP-APPENDING signal is given. Failure to give the STOP-APPENDING signal is a common source of student difficulty. The PRINT command causes the lines specified to appear on the screen of the computer terminal. The DELETE command causes the lines specified to be deleted from the buffer. Think of Ed finding the cards, removing them from the file, and destroying them.

Our computer system is a Digital Equipment Corporation PDP-11. We use the UNIX* operating system under license from Western Electric Cor-

---

*UNIX is a trademark of Bell Laboratories.

poration. UNIX was developed by Bell Telephone Laboratories, and the text editor Ed is supplied by Western Electric as the standard editor to be used with the system. UNIX is an excellent system; my negative impression of the text editor does not apply to the quality of the UNIX system as a whole. But the design philosophy of UNIX is badly matched to the needs of the everyday user. It is a system for experts. Although we studied Ed, we ourselves stopped using it the instant we could find a substitute—and people all over the country obliged by constructing alternate versions. Alas, each "improvement" has corrected some problems at the cost of introducing new ones.

In Chapter 19 I shall comment on system design and the lack of concern for the psychology of the user.

In our experimental situation we asked students to learn by doing: by actually using the text editor, referring to an instruction manual for guidance, and discovering what had happened from the results that appeared on the screen of the computer terminal. We varied the manual quite a bit, sometimes using the one supplied with the system, sometimes using versions we wrote ourselves. In most of the examples that follow, we were using a very simple manual that we wrote. The basic experimental situation is shown in Figure 17-1.

The laboratory computer watched over everything. Four different programs were working simultaneously. The text-editor program, Ed, responded appropriately to whatever command a student typed on the terminal. In addition, a special program, INSTRUCT, presented the instruction manual to the student on a second terminal and made it easy for the student to go back and forth through the manual or to look at the table of contents. INSTRUCT kept a record of what the student read and for how long. The third program, SPY, watched over all that went on and kept records of everything the student typed. One of the goals of our research was to devise an automated tutoring program, and so we had a fourth program, TEACH, that used the information provided by SPY and INSTRUCT to monitor the student's progress. It was designed to be able to interrupt the student with useful advice or to call an instructor and point out the difficulty the student was currently in.

The instruction manual led the student through the basic operation of the text editor, command by command, emphasizing learning by doing. After a brief introduction, the student learned how to get new text into the computer by using the APPEND command. Next the student learned how to get the computer to type back what had just been entered by using the PRINT command. The manual then went on to more esoteric things, but I shall stop after the next stage: the process of eliminating erroneous lines from the text by using the DELETE command.

By now you may be forming an image of the system. We found that the students very quickly constructed a conceptual model of what was happening

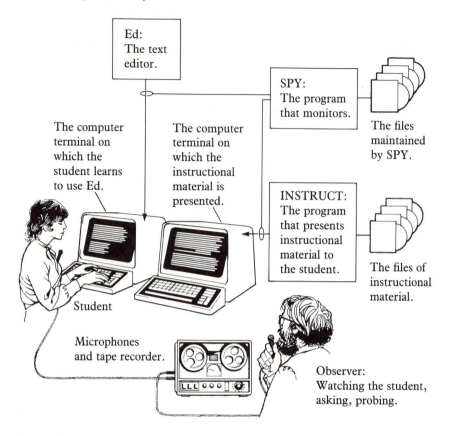

Figure 17-1.
Setup for text editor experiment.

and used it to guide their interpretation of the situation. However, because they knew virtually nothing about the operation of a computer, their initial conceptualizations were almost always wrong, which usually led to severe difficulties later on.

In the following sample learning session the Ed display screen started off blank except for the cursor, a bright square the same size as a letter. The cursor indicates the place on the screen where new material will be added. The first instructions that required action on the part of the student read:

You are going to learn how to print the text on the screen.

Type

3p

Type the key marked RETURN

(The stilted language of the text is a result of our attempts to put together a system that could be understood both by a student and by the simple English-language capability of yet another computer program we were attempting to construct: it would learn in the same way as the student by reading an identical instruction manual. Later you will see why our attempts failed.) The first instruction was clear and the students had no difficulty in following the request. The sequence "3p RETURN" is a command for Ed to print the third line of text on the screen. As a result the line from the text material that we had previously put into Ed appeared on the Ed terminal screen, making the screen look like this:

3p

this is the third line of a sample of material in the buffer.

☐

The first line on the screen is the command typed by the student. The second line is the resulting output from Ed, and the third line is the cursor. The RETURN command does not leave a mark but simply moves the cursor to the start of a new line. (Remember that the symbol <R> indicates the typing of RETURN.)

What did the student learn from the exercise? Our typical student learned that when the sequence 3p<R> is typed, the third line of the text is printed on the screen. According to our theory of learning, the student has added a schema to memory. The schema acquired consists of a goal (in this case the desire to print the third line), the action that should be performed, and the actual result. The schema for printing the third line of text, then, is a goal–action schema (GA) that looks something like this:

GA-1

    Goal: line 3 is printed on the screen

    Action: 3p<R>

    Result: the following appears on the screen:

        3p

        the text of line 3 is printed on the screen

For convenience I have switched the notation from the drawings of page 49 to the format shown here—but the two are equivalent. (The name of the

schema, GA-1, is not important; it simply allows us to refer to the schema.)
Note that it is necessary to distinguish between the goal of the schema and
the result of doing the action specified by the schema. In general, the goal
will be a subset of the result, but not always, because the result specifies
everything that happens, including by-products of the action. For example,
the characters of the command itself (3p) will also show up on the screen.
The result spells out the student's expectation of all that will happen. Thus
if later in the learning session the letters that were typed for the command
did not appear on the screen, the student would be surprised and puzzled.

The next line of the instruction manual contained a typical teacher's
admonition:

(You must always type RETURN after you have typed any command.)

The statement was added to help the student, because we had discovered
that a common error made by the beginner was to forget to type the RE-
TURN key. The student would type "3p" and then sit patiently waiting for
the computer to respond. But because of the way Ed works, nothing the
student had typed was sent to Ed until the RETURN key was typed, and so
Ed would also wait. The mutual waiting was not beneficial to the learning
process.

Our warning worked and the problem seemed to be solved. Students would
read the statement and type RETURN. But this kind of casual statement
represents bad teaching. Let me explain why, first by introducing a new form
of schema—trigger-action—(TA) then by showing how the TA schema that
results from the admonition is inadequate.

The statement "You must always type RETURN after you have typed any
command" is a prescription for action: whenever you find yourself in this
situation, do this action. We expected the student to develop a schema that
would automatically be invoked whenever a command was being typed. But
notice that the form of the GA schema is inappropriate. The GA schema is
meant to be selected whenever its goal matches the current intention. But in
this situation one needs a schema that is triggered whenever its conditions
match the current situation. We need a trigger-action schema something like
TA-100:

TA-100

Trigger: a command has just been typed.

Action: <R>

Result: unknown

Goal: unknown

In Chapter 13 I introduced the general concept of condition–action schemas, in which an action is performed once a condition is satisfied. The GA and TA schemas are special cases of condition–action schemas. In a GA schema the condition is the intention to reach a specified goal. In a TA schema the condition is the existence of a specified trigger situation.

It is fairly obvious that TA-100 restates the admonition of the instruction manual, and so TA-100 can be constructed in a straightforward way by reading the appropriate sentence in the manual (and learning by accretion). The TA looks satisfactory because it would allow students to pass an examination on the use of the RETURN key without any trouble. If asked, "When should you type the RETURN key?" the student could search his or her memory for a schema whose action was "type RETURN." That search would retrieve TA-100, and the student could reply by telling us the trigger condition: "Whenever a command has been typed." Alas, the student could pass the examination but fail to do the action at the proper time. Why? Because TA-100 is useless knowledge. The trigger has been specified in such a way that it will never be invoked.

Look back at GA-1. Is the action specified there a command? More important, does the student think of it as a command? Yes and no. Yes, GA-1 was meant to illustrate a command—the first command the student learned—but no, the student has not been told that it is a command. In fact, the student doesn't know what a command is. That word was never defined. It was first used in the parenthetical sentence about typing RETURN. We should have specified *why* RETURN was needed. That would have let the goal or purpose of RETURN be understood. But because we thought we were just giving a parenthetical suggestion, we neglected to do so. Why didn't we at least state "(Note that your typing is not sent to Ed until you press the key marked RETURN. Think of RETURN as transmitting the line. Make sure that every line you type ends with RETURN.)" Even that would not have been enough. We should have required the student to use the new schema immediately at least once, so that the actions would be performed. The schema must get encoded as actions, not words.

The problem here is with our teaching, not with TA-100. This was not discovered initially for two important reasons. First, students did not make errors, not yet. They typed RETURN, but that was because the previous line had told them to. Second, the students could answer our examination question on the typing of RETURN. Much later in the learning situation, students started making errors with RETURN. Why? It took us an amazingly long time to figure out that the problem was traceable to that early sentence, presented right at the start of the learning session and apparently understood by the students. If only the students had made known that they were puzzled and confused instead of nodding contentedly! The curse of teaching is false understanding.

Knowledge must be represented in a form appropriate to the way in which it will be used. The proper way to teach—and the proper way to test—is in a real situation, not in the artificial world of question asking.

The next part of the instruction manual was built on the following statement:

> Now try printing the fifth line.

That statement requires the student to learn by analogy. Once the student has discovered that typing the sequence 3p<R> will cause the third line from the text to appear on the screen, it is a simple matter for the student to make up a new GA schema for printing the fifth line.

GA-2

    Goal: line 5 is printed on the screen.

    Action: 5p<R>

    Result: 5p

              the text of line 5 is printed on the screen

The derivation of GA-2 illustrates learning by generalizing from one particular knowledge structure to create another. Students had no difficulty doing that. All they needed was a sufficient number of examples so that the general format could be noted. Then, schemas GA-1 and GA-2 could be generalized by substituting the concept of <line-number> everywhere a specific number occurs in the schemas. This yields GA-3:

GA-3

    Goal: <line-number> is printed on the screen

    Action: <line-number>p<R>

    Result: <line-number>p

              the text of line <line-number> is printed on the screen

This part of the instruction sequence (and of the computer model we built to read and learn from the manual) worked fine, I am pleased to say. Learning by analogy is an important learning method when the proper model is used. But as the next example demonstrates, learning by analogy can lead to difficulty if the analogy is flawed.

Consider how a student uses learning by analogy to understand the DE-LETE command. Here is the exact text of the beginning of the lesson on

DELETE from the instruction manual that was supplied to us with the UNIX system:

> Suppose we want to get rid of extra lines in the buffer. That is done by the DELETE command d. Except that d deletes commands instead of printing them, its action is similar to that of p.

That text seems simple enough. Our students would read the passage and create something like GA-10, a schema for DELETE patterned after GA-3 for PRINT. (The buffer, the student had been told, was the place where the material typed to Ed was stored as it was being worked on.)

GA-10

Goal:	<line-number> is deleted from the screen
Action:	<line-number>d<R>
Result:	<line-number>d
	the text of line <line-number> is deleted from the screen

Schema GA-10 is wrong. Yes, it will lead the student to the correct action, but then it will predict the wrong result. GA-10 states that one result of the DELETE command is that the designated line is deleted from the screen. In actuality the text stays there; nothing is deleted from the screen. Yet GA-10 seems sensible, and it describes exactly what students expect.

Here is a typical example of what happened. A student had successfully printed a five-line paragraph of text on the screen, was next instructed in the meaning of the DELETE command, and asked to delete the fourth line of the text. Having most likely formed a schema similar to GA-10, building by analogy from knowledge of the PRINT command, the student carefully typed

4d<R>

Line 4 remained in view. This was a puzzle. Why was line 4 still there? What went wrong?

A common response of students was to assume that somehow or other Ed didn't "notice" the command, and so they typed "4d<R>" once more. That action invoked the DELETE command a second time, thereby eliminating from the buffer the new line 4, which used to be line 5.

The expectations of the students were perfectly logical. More sophisticated text editors do what the students expected—when a command to delete a line is given, that line is removed from what is being displayed on the screen.

Ed, however, was designed for typewriter terminals and acts as if it were printing on paper, and so it does not change the display on the terminal screen when a line is deleted.

The error committed by the students was in part a result of their incomplete conceptualization of the various parts of the computer system. They reasoned that the screen was controlled by the computer, and so if the computer deleted a line, it should also have been deleted from the screen. This form of reasoning did not occur when the very same instruction manual and text editor were used with a typewriter terminal. The students knew the computer could not physically erase a line previously printed. The difference was in the students' mental models, not in the formal information they were receiving. Our teaching was faulty because we failed to take account of the problem of the nondisappearing line—but that was one reason we were doing the set of experiments: to learn how to teach.

We solved the problem by explaining the operation of the typewriter terminal that Ed was designed to be used on. This let the student use a new prototype and a new analogy in constructing an appropriate schema for the DELETE command. But our explanation did not cover all that happens when the DELETE command is used. Eventually the student has to realize that several texts are being edited. There is the text being displayed on the screen of the terminal. There is also the text being held in the buffer memory of Ed. Finally, there is the disk file of the computer where the results of the editing session are stored. What is visible on the screen is not necessarily what is in Ed's text buffer or for that matter what is stored permanently in the computer's disk files.

When Ed is commanded to delete a line, it deletes that line from its buffer. It does not change what is on the screen or what is on the permanent files of the computer. To update the screen, Ed must be given a PRINT command; to update the disk file, Ed must be given a WRITE command.

Before beginning students can understand the DELETE command properly, they must first get a large increment in their understanding of computer systems. The students must establish their first conceptualization of the distinctions among the parts of the computer. They must learn that the computer has several kinds of memory. They must realize that the terminal is not the computer but an independent device with its own local memory of what is on the screen. Finally, they must learn that Ed is simply one of many programs that use the computer and that the operations of Ed must be distinguished from those of the terminal and those of the computer system.

To make Ed understandable, we needed to give the students an appropriate conceptual model of the text-editing process. The difficulty, though, was that our students knew nothing about computers, so either our model was going to be incomplete, or we were going to have to spend considerable time giving them the complete model. We discovered an interesting solution to this dilemma: give the students many different conceptual models, each one simple, each making a different point.

Earlier in this chapter, I discussed the operation of the text editor, explaining that it was something like a combination of a secretary and a card file. These are two separate conceptual models that we presented to our students. A third model is a tape recorder.

The secretarial model explains some aspects of Ed, especially the overall format of intermixing commands and text material. The difficulty with the model, however, was that our students expected Ed to be as intelligent and understanding as a real secretary would be. Hence if they gave the APPEND command, they then fell prey to what we call "the append-mode trap." They would append text but fail to tell Ed when they had finished appending. Instead they would issue a new command and expect Ed to carry it out. Ed, of course, would treat the command as another line of text and simply add it to the file. But, because Ed often gets commands and follows them without giving any visible reaction, the students were sometimes unaware of what had happened. This led to distressing problems. The situation is analogous to the business executive who says the following to her secretary:

> Please take a memo. The aforementioned shipment of yours re June 17 has been received without prejudice until test-bed configurations are confirmed. Is there any coffee? Predicted completion of configuration tests is July 15. Sincerely, et cetera.

A secretary would not include the question "Is there any coffee?" in the memo, but Ed takes everything literally. Ed has to be told:

> . . . until test-bed configurations are confirmed. Stop dictation. Is there any coffee? Resume dictation. Predicted completion. . . .

So the secretarial model has some virtues and some difficulties. The tape-recorder model helps students to understand the append-mode trap. Think of Ed as a tape recorder, they are told, and think of the APPEND command as equivalent to recording on the tape recorder. Once a tape recorder has been put into the record mode, it faithfully records every sound that reaches its microphones. The only way to stop the recording is to perform the explicit action that terminates the record mode (usually by pushing the lever marked *stop*).

The tape-recorder model takes care of the append-mode trap, but it does not explain the DELETE command.

The file-card model offers a good analogy for understanding the line-oriented structure of the records kept by Ed. Thus the renumbering of lines that takes place after a DELETE or APPEND command is completed is easy to interpret, given the model of the removal or addition of cards in a file. As you have already seen, however, the file-card model by itself does not explain why the deleted line is not removed from the text the student sees on the screen. But it does provide the proper conceptual framework. An appropriate interpretation of the situation is that the contents of the file cards are not visible to the user of Ed. Those are Ed's private files. If you want to know what is in the files, you must ask to see them with a PRINT command.

The use of such models provides an important supplement to our arsenal of teaching strategies. We have found that students make up their own conceptualizations anyway, and if we don't give them guidance, their models can be bizarre and difficult to overcome. The worst aspect of the student's own creations is that they often seem to provide a good explanation of what has been happening. Thus neither the student nor the instructor realizes how bad the model is, and it is not until the model leads to some major difficulty that a hint of basic trouble develops. By then the true problem may lie far away in the past, and only the most patient teachers will be able to unravel the cause of the present difficulty.

18

Some Reflections on Learning

People actively construct mental models of the situations they are in. This is true of all events—conversations with friends, the reading of novels, attempts to learn new subjects, or any other endeavors.

I have introduced simplified formalisms—GA and TA schemas—for representing the construction of mental models. In principle, by employing a sufficient number of schemas worked through in sufficient detail, one could follow changes in the knowledge structures of a person learning a subject.

The proposal I have advanced suggests that schemas can contain both general knowledge and knowledge about actions. Schemas are activated either conceptually, by seeing a specific goal (GA schemas), or through data-driven processes, by triggering specific patterns (TA schemas). In this proposal, the formation of schemas by copying old ones and making appropriate changes or by filling in empty data areas in existing schemas is essentially the process of learning through accretion.

Learning through structuring involves the generation of new conceptualizations and therefore of new formats for schemas. In the example of the Ed program, I stopped the analysis just prior to the restructuring the student goes through in the development of an understanding of the DELETE command.

Tuning, in this proposal, is the refinement of specific TA's and GA's. Frequently used command sequences become integrated into single patterns, actions become more efficient, schemas develop for shortcuts or for specialized requests and special circumstances.

In this book I have provided just a hint of the total model of learning. Psychologists are still far from understanding the mechanics of the mind. The various proposals for representational and computational schemes put forward in recent years all offer new insights, yet all of them fail to yield a satisfactory model of human behavior. Still, the spirit of my particular model is the spirit of most contemporary work being done in cognitive science on the development of computer-simulation models of human behavior. Note too that the schema structures do provide some insight into the conceptual errors made by students as they progressed through the instruction manual.

One thing my colleagues and I learned as we constructed our model was the rather unbelievable detail in which we had to examine the learning process and with which we had to explore the students' background knowledge. One of my colleagues—Ross Bott—spent months examining how the students' prior knowledge about television sets, typewriters, and computers affected their learning of Ed. To understand the students' problems with the DELETE command, one has to understand the students' expectations about the power of computers. Most students have only fragmentary knowledge of computers and usually impart to them powers and intelligence far in excess of their real capabilities. A successful model of learning must also encompass erroneous information.

We were at first dismayed by the numerous learning difficulties our computer model faced and the numerous conceptual ambiguities it discovered as it attempted to understand the instruction manual. Its difficulties caused us to take a closer look at the behavior of students in the same situation, and to our surprise, we found similar numbers and types of problems. Instruction manuals we had written with great care to be clear and precise turned out to be vague or misleading when they were subjected to the microscopic gaze of our schema-based analysis. Students tend to shrug off problems, however, passing over contradictions in the text or gaps and inconsistencies in their own knowledge without much hesitation. This is a useful strategy, because if our most carefully prepared texts are bad, presumably most of the instructional material in the world is even worse. People would never learn anything if they needed to understand everything well before they could continue.

Learning is often an act of interpretation—past knowledge is brought to bear; past experiences help to determine current expectations. A learner builds a framework of knowledge understanding that is consistent with the particular aspects of the task that seem most relevant. Like an iceberg, this structure has its most essential features hidden from view (Figure 18-1). The structure may not be at all what the teacher intended, but careful analysis of

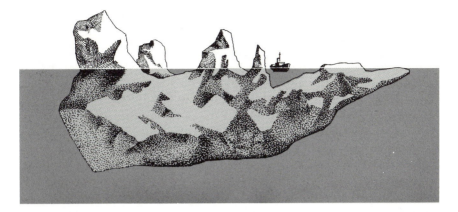

Figure 18-1.
The iceberg metaphor of learning and teaching.

From the point of view of the learner: The student observes the material and events visible at the surface. The student must then postulate some underlying structure to explain what has been observed. The problem is that numerous underlying structures can be postulated to fit the constraints imposed by the observations.

From the point of view of the teacher: The teacher observes the student, attempts to determine what the student knows, and investigates the source of any difficulties. Unfortunately, the teacher has access to only a limited set of observations about the student, represented by the material above the surface. The teacher must postulate some underlying knowledge structure to explain what the student does. The problem is that numerous underlying structures can be postulated, and the peaks do not at all reflect the complexity of the student's underlying knowledge structure.

the students' hypotheses and of the explanations of the origins of these hypotheses reveals that the ideas inherent in the structure are consistent with the evidence so far offered the student. The problem is that the early stages of instruction in a new topic often do not have sufficient constraints to direct the learner's hypotheses in appropriate directions.

With any new topic there is a huge amount that must be learned, much of it depending on the existence of appropriate knowledge structures within the learner. No wonder learning normally takes time and is often difficult. No wonder apprentices at such disparate tasks as bricklaying, plumbing, surgery, and newspaper reporting need years of experience before they can perform with facility. No wonder an adult who wishes to learn about the science of nuclear reactors or about international finance, or who wishes to acquire a second language can easily become overwhelmed by the huge size of such a task and experience strong feelings of incompetence.

Look up an advanced science course in a university catalogue and you will probably discover that several other courses are required as prerequisites; those too are likely to have prerequisites. Even though the catalogue may not say so explicitly, these courses may require advanced calculus or probability theory; these in turn require elementary analysis and differential equations, which in turn assume a basic knowledge of algebra, geometry, and trigonometry. What person learning a second language can give it anywhere near the amount of time spent learning the first, native language? Earlier I stated that close to 5000 hours would be required to become an expert. This chapter indicates why so many hours might be needed.

Professional musicians usually started the serious study of music when they were very young. People who are superior mechanics have most likely been exposed to mechanical devices and to the active construction (and destruction) of things since early childhood. I have actively studied and practiced cooking for approximately 10 years, but I consider myself to be a good cook for only a limited set of cuisines and dishes. In our culture the skills attributed primarily to men or to women have been arbitrarily assigned. It is true that assignments have sometimes changed over the past century as women take on men's traditional jobs and men take on women's. But sexual stereotyping still obtains when it comes to tasks such as mechanics and sports, sewing and cooking, science and humanities, and such stereotyping reflects the early training and experiences of the young child. The huge amount of detailed structure involved in becoming an expert almost demands that the learning begin when a person is young and continue for many years, perhaps even for life. New knowledge often builds on old knowledge. The more one knows, the easier it is to learn more.

19

The Human Use
of Human Beings

As I wrote this book I observed my environment, especially the part of it created by modern technology. My intention was to collect examples that would show how the material of the book was relevant to everyday life. I was pleasantly surprised to find that as my work progressed, the relevance seemed to expand. But the most striking examples came from examining the design of systems meant to be used by or for people. I was forced to conclude that system designers misuse and ignore people's capabilities.

It is surprising how badly technology matches human capabilities. People are flexible, amazingly so. The range of our abilities is immense. We manage and cope with a wide variety of circumstances. Those who design and construct the tools of modern society, however, seem to have little understanding of our capabilities. As a result, we are slaves to technology. We make errors, and like the students I studied, we assume it is natural and proper to do so. If we get upset about the errors, we are upset at ourselves for being so stupid or forgetful. Nonsense.

I have made a collection of the errors people make. For instance, they put the top of the sugar bowl on a coffee cup, turn off the automobile engine when they mean to turn off the windshield wipers, or try to make coffee without adding water. Such errors are humorous. Sometimes they are frustrating. But some errors are potentially serious: a system malfunction at the Three Mile Island nuclear power plant (March 28, 1979) may possibly have been aggravated by two auxiliary feedwater valves that had been closed for service and were never reopened. I claim that such errors are not the fault of the operators; they are system-induced errors. The design of the system ignored the principles discussed in this book, guaranteeing that the error would happen. And so I write this chapter, in part to illuminate the relevance of the material in the book to everyday life, in part to help reverse the design faults of technology. The title of the chapter, "The Human Use of Human Beings," is borrowed from Norbert Weiner's perceptive analysis, in 1950.

If you get the chance, examine the control room of an electricity-generating nuclear power plant. Impressive, isn't it? All those dials and knobs, switches and lights. Did you ever wonder how the plant operators manage? Do wonder. The design of the control panel is a combination of chance, luck, incompatible components, and almost complete indifference to the problems of human functioning on the part of the people who specify the plant. A typical control room has more than 100 feet of panels, as many as 3000 meters and controls (with some meters requiring ladders or footstools to be read), and other meters or alarms located tens of feet away from the relevant controls, all seemingly designed as if to maximize memory load and to minimize an operator's ability to match actual plant functioning to an internal, mental model of proper functioning.

Such systems tax the memories of even the most highly trained operators. The proper solution is to redesign the system. The current solution is to provide aids to memory in the form of reference manuals that are organized for the convenience of the system, not of the user. I have examined some of the flight reference manuals published by commercial airlines. They are not easy to use in an emergency. What is needed is organization and referencing by function. Instead there is organization by form or by fiat. Where are the principles of memory structure, of memory retrieval? And where does one put manuals when they are needed? In modern systems there is no place to put the manuals without obscuring controls. I have watched pilots of commuter planes struggle to find a spot for their half-filled coffee cups, try to keep up with multiple radio signals, and carry on necessary conversations with their crew—all the while consulting course and landing instructions on hand-lettered check-off lists taped to the windows, the panels, the visors.

There are people who know how to do better. There are designers and human-factors engineers (along with societies and journals such as *Human Factors* and *Ergonomics*) who do worry about these issues. But the actual designers of equipment tend to dismiss their craft as "mere common sense." Moreover, they see the worriers as nuisances, asking for experiments on proposed systems, trying them out before they are completely designed, all of which takes time and costs money. Yet there is more to design than common sense. It is not a matter of deciding how best to design a switch or a meter; it is a matter of trying to understand the functioning of the human, of deciding whether a switch or meter ought to be present at all. A design should center on the functions and intentions of the human. It shouldn't force the human to match the arbitrary needs of the machine. System designers should start by considering the user. All too often they start with the machine, and the human is not thought of until the end, when it's too late: witness the control panels in the nuclear power plants.

Consider the text-editing system I described earlier. Ed is a horrible piece of cognitive engineering. It offers no way of letting the user know in what mode the system is operating, save by remembering. But remembering places a heavy burden on short-term memory, especially when the person who is editing is in a noisy office environment where telephones are ringing, where it is often necessary to leave the desk, and where many other normal interruptions and distractions of the day are going on.

Is the taxing of short-term memory limited to that text editor? Not at all. There are displays designed for aircraft pilots that have the same problem (especially those new, powerful computer displays—powerful and dangerous). And how about your automobile? Do you always remember the setting of the headlight switch or the emergency brake? (You mean you have never left the headlights on all day or tried to drive with the emergency brake on?) Have you never driven forward when you meant to go in reverse? How about driving someone else's car and trying to find the lights, the horn, or the windshield-wiper control?

What has my tirade to do with this book? A lot. My goal was to introduce you to the study of human information-processing mechanisms, most especially those mechanisms that are involved in memory and learning. Along the way I discussed sensory memory, primary and secondary memory, and some of the issues concerning the use of memory structures: how stuff once stored away can ever be retrieved. I spoke of networks and schemas, descriptions and search strategies. In the study of learning I discussed the way in which performance changes as one progresses from beginning to expert knowledge, and in the examination of understanding I showed that the learner builds an internal model of the topic being learned, a model that helps piece together and make sense out of the otherwise disparate pieces of the subject matter. When they are put together, the chapters deal with the human system, with the mechanisms available for cognitive functioning and with the variety of skills and levels of performance.

I passed over other aspects of human performance. An important one is people in society. People do not operate as isolated entities. We exist within a physical environment, within a society, within a culture. The environment and the society and the culture play important parts in our performance.

Take memory, especially the well-known (but seldom heeded) limitations of human short-term memory. We can keep active only so much material at any one time. Distractions tend to cause loss of that material. It is all very plainly stated in those nice, neat laboratory results shown in the early part of this book. But the demands of modern life ignore such simple concerns. The overloading of air-traffic controllers is well known, but there are other, less specialized situations. The harried automobile driver, driving on unfamiliar roads, late for an appointment, watching traffic, must cope with those ever-present unintelligible and semivisible road signs. Add high-quality stereophonic sound from built-in, high-quality tape recorders, and you have guaranteed distraction from the primary task of driving, guaranteed overload of conscious mental abilities.

The environment is an important part of our memory for just the kinds of problems I have called mode errors. We retain the state or mode of our operations, sometimes internally, but most often externally. I don't have to remember what task I'm doing as long as I'm doing it; the position of my body and the objects in the environment serve as a memory. The pile of papers on the left-hand corner of my table is my memory stack of things to do; the pile just adjacent to it is the memory stack of things I intend to take to the university. Those external piles of papers are just as much a part of my active working-memory system as is my internal primary-memory store. Modern computer technology is removing the support of the environment from our memory usage. A modern computer control system has one simple television screen. Erase part of the display on the screen when space is needed for something else and the external memory is erased. That sounds like a simple point, but it is not. Erasure can have profound consequences.

Society and culture interact with us in multiple ways, determining much of our knowledge and how we use that knowledge. Our culture pervades our cognitive functioning. Use so-called culture-free American memory materials to test native Africans who have not been to school, and you will get miserable performances. Test those same people with materials and situations from their own culture, and you will get good performance. (Test educated Americans with African materials and you will get miserable performance.)

The human is a system of interacting components. Within each of us there are many cognitive mechanisms interacting with one another, interacting with emotions and motivations, with intentions and goals, and with the biological systems and physical parts of the body. Each person also interacts with a complex sociocultural setting. Anyone who attempts to design devices that take into account human functioning must consider all aspects, from the details of short-term memory and attentional limitations to the interactions of human, machine, and society. It will not suffice simply to design a knob to match human requirements; the whole system must be designed to take into account the whole human being.

The earlier discussion of the learning of complex skills offered other lessons that must be heeded. Such skills take considerable time to acquire, with considerable demands on background knowledge—the prior understanding of the person. That is why people with other cultural backgrounds find it difficult to work with technology from our culture. That is why many people seem unable to learn mathematics—gaps in their background knowledge make mathematical concepts unintelligible. Our culture emphasizes and reinforces that mathematics is "hard."

Because complex skills require knowledge and memory as well as performance abilities, beginners are slow and awkward, in need of continual guidance, whereas professionals are experts able to whiz through with speed, accuracy, and minimum effort. A designer must think of both the beginner and the expert simultaneously. The expert wants a simple system with a minimum of intrusion in terms of help and prompting and extra responses. The beginner needs continual prompting, reassurance, extra responses that confirm or allow for a change of mind. To design one system for all classes of users is not easy, but it must be done.

The underlying conceptual structure of a system must be made obvious, allowing the user to work with the system, to understand the rationale behind seemingly arbitrary responses. Even false conceptual structures are useful if they map nicely onto the system operation. But to ignore conceptual structure, to make it look arbitrary and capricious, leads to difficulty in usage, to error, to dangerous situations. If a digital watch is hard to use, people will stop buying it soon enough. "It takes an engineering degree to change the time," one disgruntled user told me when I asked about his shiny new watch. The same watch, properly designed, would not be so difficult to use. When it comes to modern automobiles, home washing machines, or industrial products, however, difficulties may lead to catastrophes.

Once I argued that it was time for a new discipline: cognitive engineering. At that time I was thinking of education, of the problems of teaching and tutoring, of automated instructional systems. Now, with a wider perception of the need to make technology our friend and ally, not our enemy, I think the time for such a discipline has more than come.

We are entering a new era of technology in which cheap computer power will be widely available. Computer power can be used either to our advantage or to our disadvantage. It can be used to depersonalize life, making us slaves to machines, to the arbitrary whims of the computer programmer who likes precise, neat forms. Or it can be used to make life pleasant, more flexible and adaptable. With increased computer use we could have mass-produced objects built to individual specifications. We could receive just the news that we wish to see and hear, the television that we wish to experience. Libraries could be more widely accessible. Intellectual resources could be more widely distributed. Education could be fun, with interesting games, full of insight, readily available in the home, giving individually tailored tutorial coaching. But all that is possible only if intelligence is used in the design of the systems from the very beginning. That intelligence must first be applied to understanding how people remember and learn.

Guide to Further Reading

General Readings

For those who wish to read more about the topics covered in this book, let me suggest further reading. An excellent survey of the entire field of Cognitive Science is provided in Morton Hunt's book *The universe within: A new science explores the human mind* (Hunt, 1982). This is a popular book, aimed at the general reader, which provides broad coverage, while remaining very readable and authoritative.

For a more technical, though readily understandable, approach, I recommend three textbooks. My text *Memory and attention* (Norman, 1976) provides an introduction to the topics, combining excerpts (heavily edited) from the literature, along with my comments and opinions. My undergraduate text, *Human information processing* (Lindsay and Norman, 1977) is both more elementary and more thorough; it gives a general overview of many topics, far more than are included in this book. Then, for a treatment slightly more advanced, I recommend John Anderson's text, *Cognitive psychology and its implications* (Anderson, 1980). For the most advanced treatment, see the six-volume *Handbook of learning and cognitive processes* edited by Estes (1978). Volumes 4, *Attention and Memory*, and 5, *Human Information Processing*, are the most relevant.

Readings On Memory

The structure of human memory provides good introductions and essays (Cofer, 1976) and Kilhstrom and Evans' (1979) *Functional disorders of memory* discusses other important aspects of memory. Work on semantic memory grew out of the notions of Ross Quillian in the 1960s (Quillian, 1968, 1969), some of which is reviewed in texts by Anderson (1980) and by Lindsay and Norman (1976). Our own further work is presented in advanced detail in the book by Norman, Rumelhart, and the LNR Research Group, *Explorations in cognition* (1975). I highly recommend Neisser's *Memory observed: Remembering in natural contexts* (1982). This is a naturalistic approach to the study of memory, the investigation of how remembering and forgetting take place in the everyday world outside the psychological laboratory.

Problems in representation have played important roles in both Artificial Intelligence and Psychology, and the books edited by Bobrow and Collins (1975) and Rosch and Lloyd (1978) provide good discussions of these issues. A review of the entire area is provided in the *Handbook of artificial intelligence* (Barr and Feigenbaum, 1981). To get an appreciation of the tremendous amount of knowledge that must be represented to understand even such a simple task as painting a wall, see the story by Charniak (1977) about his attempts to represent that knowledge.

The discussion in this book on the role of descriptions is my own, reported in Norman and Bobrow (1979). The protocols on retrieval of names of classmates from the past is reported in Williams and Hollan (1981). Schemas are not well described in this book, but they are important in my thinking, and the thinking of others in the field. An important paper on the closely related concept of "frames" is by Minsky (1975), and one version of the paper can be found in Johnson-Laird and Wason (1977). Other discussions can be found in papers my colleagues and I have written: Norman and Bobrow (Cofer, 1976); Rumelhart and Norman (1978); and Rumelhart and Ortony (1977). The book by Schank and Abelson (1977) presents a different, but useful organizational structure—that of scripts; and a simple introduction appears in the Johnson-Laird and Wason book (1977). Further discussions on memory structures can be found in Schank's paper in *Perspectives on Cognitive Science* (Norman, 1981).

There are several sources for discussions of mental imagery. An interesting overview is provided by Richardson (1969). Perhaps the most thorough and interesting of the modern treatments is that of Steve Kosslyn (1981). An interesting set of articles on imagery is provided in the last section of Johnson-Laird and Wason. My discussion on judging directions was based on work done by Stevens and Coupe (1978). You will get a good idea of the complexity of thought on the topic of imagery if you examine the "treatment" of the paper by Kosslyn, Pinker, Smith, and Schwartz (1980) in the very interesting journal *The behavioral and brain sciences*. When it publishes a paper it includes commentaries by many of the major workers in the field, who state why they agree or disagree with the arguments made within the paper. It makes for lively reading, and is a good way to become familiar with the debates within science.

Not much is known about additive memories, for this is a relatively new development. The best treatment is provided in Hinton and Anderson (1981). There are surprisingly few reviews of more conventional (place) memories relevant to the discussion in this book, however, I recommend the chapter by Winograd, in the Cofer book.

Problem Solving and Skilled Performance

Thinking: Readings in cognitive science, an excellent book edited by Johnson-Laird and Wason (1977), covers thought and problem solving, thereby covering much that is relevant to this book. If you read only the introductions to each part, you will have an excellent up-to-date course on thinking.

There is surprisingly little on learning and on skilled performance, at least from the point of view that I have represented within this book. Excellent reviews of skilled human performance are provided in the chapter by Fitts (1964), the books by Welford (1968, 1976), and in Fitts and Posner (1967). The studies of cigar making (performed by Crossman), telegraph code learning, and learning over many trials are reported in these references. The telegraphy work was done by Bryan and Harter (1897, 1899), but I must warn you that Keller (1958) denied the existence of learning plateaus and questioned the accuracy of the Bryan and Harter studies. The age of these references reflects the relative lack of concern for skilled performance in contemporary cognitive psychology. I would like to believe that things are changing, and that skilled performance is again coming under extensive investigation. See, for example, the collection of papers in Stelmach (1978) and in Stelmach and Requin (1980), and in the book *Cognitive skills and their acquisition,* edited by John Anderson (1981). Hatano, Miyake, and Binks (1977) performed the experiments and observations on skilled abacus users.

The discussion of accretion, structuring, and tuning comes from my work with Rumelhart (Rumelhart and Norman, 1978, 1981); we used the term "restructuring" to emphasize the change in existing structures.

Learning

Much of the work reported on our studies involving the text editor Ed has been performed with the collaboration of my colleagues and students in the LNR research laboratory at the University of California, San Diego, and the work and ideas reported in this book are jointly developed and performed. At the moment, very little has been published, however. The thesis by Bott (1979), which studies the problems involved in the learning of the text editor, is quite relevant, but as yet, unpublished. Bott develops some of the issues of representation, with emphasis upon strategies and the tremendous amount of prior and acquired knowledge that is necessary to the learning of complex materials—the iceberg problem.

The study of learning and of automated tutorial devices has the potential to dramatically affect the educational process: a few simple notions of the sort discussed here, coupled with intelligent tutorial strategies can create powerful teaching devices by means of relatively small contemporary mini-and micro-computers. Some of these intelligent tutoring machines are discussed in a special issue of the *International Journal of Man–Machine Studies,* January 1979 (vol. 11, no. 1, pp. 1–156: Sleeman and Brown, 1979). See also Gentner (1979) and O'Neil (1979).

One approach to the problem of figuring out a student's problems or "bugs," especially when the difficulty reveals itself quite far removed from the original source of the problem, is provided in a study of "bugs" in elementary arithmetic (Brown and Burton, 1978). Similar topics with regard to tutoring (by the Socratic method) and other issues can be found in papers by Stevens, Collins, and Goldin and by Goldstein, all in the special issue edited by Sleeman and Brown.

The report of the conference edited by Snow, Frederica, and Montague (1979) contains some good discussions, including the use of metaphors in learning and teaching, imagery, and tutorial instruction. The book *Mental models*, edited by Gentner and Stevens (1982), is also quite relevant. Finally, it can be fun to skim the journals, looking for items that will be of interest. The best journals to examine for the topics discussed in this book are: *Cognition and Instruction* (a new journal); *Brain and Behavioral Sciences; Cognitive Psychology; Cognitive Science; International Journal of Man-machine Studies; Journal of Experimental Psychology: General; Journal of Experimental Psychology: Human Perception and Performance; Journal of Experimental Psychology: Learning, Memory, and Cognition; Psychological Review.*

References

Anderson, J. R. *Language, memory, and thought*. Hillsdale, N. J.: Erlbaum, 1976.

Anderson, J. R. *Cognitive psychology and its implications*. San Francisco: W. H. Freeman and Company, 1980.

Anderson, J. R. (Ed.). *Cognitive skills and their acquisition*. Hillsdale, N. J.: Erlbaum, 1981.

Barr, A., and Feigenbaum, E. A. *The handbook of artificial intelligence*. Los Altos, Calif.: William Kaufmann, 1981.

Blackburn, J. M. Acquisition of skills: An analysis of learning curves. *Great Britain: Industrial Health Research Board Report*, (No. 73). London: H. M. S. O., 1936.

Bobrow, D. G., and Collins, A. M. (Eds.). *Representation and understanding: Studies in cognitive science*. New York: Academic Press, 1975.

Bott, R. A. *A study of complex learning, theory and methodologies*. Unpublished doctoral dissertation, University of California, San Diego, 1978.

Brown, J. S., and Burton, R. R. Diagnostic models for procedural bugs in basic mathematical skills. *Cognitive Science*, 1978, vol. 2, pp. 155–192.

Bryan, W. L., and Harter, N. Studies on the physiology and psychology of the telegraph language: The acquisition of a hierarchy of habits. *Psychological Review*, 1897, vol. 4, pp. 27–53.

Bryan, W. L., and Harter, N. Studies of the acquisition of a hierarchy of habits. *Psychological Review*, 1899, vol. 6, pp. 345–375.

Charniak, E. A framed painting: The representation of a common sense knowledge fragment. *Cognitive Science,* 1977, vol. 1, pp. 355–394.

Cofer, C. (Ed.). *The structure of human memory.* San Francisco: W. H. Freeman and Company, 1976.

Crossman, E. R. F. W. A theory of the acquisition of speed-skill. *Ergonomics,* 1959, vol. 2, pp. 153–166.

Estes, W. K. (Ed.). *Handbook of learning and cognitive processes* (6 vols.). Hillsdale, N. J.: Erlbaum, 1978.

Fitts, P. M. Perceptual-motor skill learning. In A. W. Melton (Ed.), *Categories of human learning.* New York: Academic Press, 1964.

Fitts, P. M., and Posner, M. I. *Human performance.* Belmont, Calif.: Brooks/Cole, 1967.

Gentner, D., and Stevens, A. L. (Eds.). *Mental models.* Hillsdale, N. J.: Erlbaum, 1982.

Hatano, G., Miyake, Y., and Binks, M. G. Performance of expert abacus operators. *Cognition,* 1977, vol. 5, pp. 51–71.

Hinton, G., and Anderson, J. (Eds.). *Parallel models of associative memory.* Hillsdale, N. J.: Erlbaum, 1981.

Hunt, Morton. *The universe within: A new science explores the human mind.* New York: Simon & Schuster, 1982.

Johnson-Laird, P.N., and Wason, P.C., (Eds.). *Thinking: Readings in cognitive science.* N.Y.: Cambridge University Press, 1977.

Keller, F.S. The phantom plateau. *Journal of Experimental Analysis of Behavior,* 1958, vol. 1, pp. 1–13.

Kihlstrom, J. F., and Evans, F. J., (Eds.). *Functional disorders of memory.* Hillsdale, N. J.: Erlbaum, 1979.

Kosslyn, S. M. *Image and mind.* Cambridge, Mass.: Harvard University Press, 1980.

Kosslyn, S. M., Pinker, S., Smith, G., and Shwartz, S. P. On the demystification of mental imagery. *The Behavioral and Brain Sciences,* 1979, vol. 2, pp. 535–581.

Lindsay, P. H., and Norman, D. A. *Human information processing* (2nd ed.). New York: Academic Press, 1977.

Minsky, M. A framework for representing knowledge. In P. H. Winston (Ed.), *The psychology of computer vision.* New York: McGraw-Hill, 1975.

Murdock, B. B., Jr. The serial effect of free recall. *Journal of Experimental Psychology,* 1962, vol. 64, pp. 482–488.

Neisser, U. *Memory observed: Remembering in natural contexts.* San Francisco: W.H. Freeman and Company, 1982.

Norman, D. A. *Memory and attention: An introduction to human information processing,* 2nd ed. New York: Wiley, 1976.

Norman, D. A. Twelve issues for cognitive science. In D. A. Norman (Ed.). *Perspectives on cognitive science.* Norwood, N.J.: Ablex and Hillsdale, N.J.: Erlbaum, 1981.

Norman, D. A., and Bobrow, D. G. Descriptions: An intermediate stage in memory retrieval. *Cognitive Psychology*, 1979, vol. 11, pp. 107–123.

Norman, D. A., and Rumelhart, D. E. Memory and knowledge. In D. A. Norman, D. E. Rumelhart, and The LNR Research Group, *Explorations in cognition*. San Francisco: W. H. Freeman and Company, 1975.

O'Neil, Jr., H.F. (Ed.). *Procedures for instructional systems development*. New York: Academic Press, 1979.

Postman, L., and Phillips, L. W. Short-term temporal changes in free recall. *Quarterly Journal of Experimental Psychology*, 1965, vol. 17, pp. 132–138.

Quillian, M. R. Semantic memory. In M. Minsky (Ed.), *Semantic information processing*. Cambridge, Mass.: MIT Press, 1968.

Quillian, M. R. The teachable language comprehender. *Communications of the Association for Computing Machinery*, 1969, vol. 12, pp. 459–475.

Richardson, A. *Mental imagery*. New York: Springer, 1969.

Rosch, E., and Lloyd, B. B. (Eds.). *Cognition and categorization*. Hillsdale, N. J.: Erlbaum, 1978.

Ruger, H. A. The psychology of efficiency. *Archives of Psychology*. 1910, *19*, 15.

Rumelhart, D. E., and Norman, D. A. Accretion, tuning and restructuring: Three modes of learning. In J. W. Cotton, and R. Klatzky (Eds.), *Semantic factors in cognition*. Hillsdale, N. J.: Erlbaum, 1978.

Rumelhart, D. E., and Norman, D. A. Analogical processes in learning. In J. R. Anderson (Ed.), *Cognitive skills and their acquisition*. Hillsdale, N. J.: Erlbaum, 1981.

Rumelhart, D. E., and Ortony, A. The representation of knowledge in memory. In R. C. Anderson, R. J. Spiro, and W. E. Montague (Eds.), *Schooling and the acquisition of knowledge*. Hillsdale, N. J.: Erlbaum, 1977.

Schank, R., and Abelson, R. *Scripts, plans, goals and understanding: An inquiry into human knowledge structures*. Hillsdale, N. J.: Erlbaum, 1977.

Schank, R. C., and Abelson, R. P. Scripts, plans, and knowledge. In P. N. Johnson-Laird, and P. C. Wason (Eds.), *Thinking: Readings in cognitive science*. N.Y.: Cambridge University Press, 1977.

Seibel, R. Discriminative reaction time for a 1,023 alternative task. *Journal of Experimental Psychology*, 1963, vol. 66, pp. 215–226.

Sleeman, D. H., and Brown, J. S. (Eds.). *Intelligent tutoring systems*. Special issue of *International Journal of Man-Machine Studies*, 1979, vol. 11, pp. 1–156.

Snow, R. E., Frederico, P. A., and Montague, W. E. (Eds.). *Aptitude learning and instruction: Cognitive process analyses*. Hillsdale, N.J.: Erlbaum, 1979.

Sperling, G. The information available in brief visual presentations. *Psychological Monographs*, 1960, vol. 74, pp. 1–29.

Stelmach, G. E. (Ed.). *Information processing in motor control and learning*. New York: Academic Press, 1978.

Stelmach, G. E., and Requin, J. (Eds.). *Tutorials in motor behavior*. N.Y.: North-Holland, 1980.

Stevens, A., and Coupe, P. Distortions in judged spatial relations. *Cognitive Psychology*, 1978, vol. 10, pp. 422–437.

Welford, A. T. *Fundamentals of skill*. London: Methuen Press, 1968.

Welford, A. T. *Skilled performance*. Glenview, Ill.: Scott, Foresman, 1976.

Williams, M. D., and Hollan, J. D. The process of retrieval from very long-term memory. *Cognitive Science*, 1981, vol. 5, pp. 87–119.

Index